How the Child's Mind Develops

David Cohen

Routledge
Taylor & Francis Group

HOVE AND NEW YORK

KU-595-511

First published 2002
by Routledge
27 Church Rd, Hove, E Sussex, BN3 2FA

http://www.psypress.co.uk

Simultaneously published in the USA and Canada
by Taylor & Francis Inc
29 West 35th Street, New York, NY 10001

Reprinted 2003

Routledge is an imprint of the Taylor & Francis Group

Typeset in Times by Keystroke,
Jacaranda Lodge, Wolverhampton
Printed and bound in Great Britain by
T.J. International, Padstow, Cornwall

Cover photography © Sebastian Kusenberg
(from PLAYING LIFE, Jovis Verlag, Berlin 1998)
Design: Lisa Dynan

British Library Cataloguing-in-Publication Data
A catalogue record for this book is available from the British Library

Library of Congress Cataloging-in-Publication Data

Cohen, David, 1946–
    How the child's mind develops / David Cohen.
        p. cm.
    Includes bibliographical references and index.
    ISBN 0–415–21653–2 – ISBN 0–415–21654–0 (pbk.)
    1. Cognition in children. 2. Cognition in infants. 3. Cognition in
    adolescence.
    I. Title

BF723.C5 C6363 2001
155.4'13–dc21   2001034976

ISBN 0–415–21653–2 (hbk)
ISBN 0–415–21654–0 (pbk)

Contents

Illustrations

to Aaron Cohen

Introduction

Most psychologists, when they think of thinking, speak of 'cognition' thanks to the seventeenth-century French philosopher, René Descartes. Contemplating his wood burning stove, Descartes came up with one of the sharpest slogans of all time.

cogito ergo sum
Latin for: I think therefore I am.

Cogito – hence cognition, cognitive, cogitate, all words that mean thinking or thought.

Elegant as Descartes' formula was, it makes as much sense if you run it backwards:

I am, therefore, I think.

Human beings cannot help thinking. You may be thinking rubbish, you may be thinking about nothing more than the possibility of Kansas City bidding for the next Olympics but, even so, your brain isn't totally empty.

No one is truly an airhead unless they're brain-dead.

I don't think of myself as a thinking sort of person. Quite. But you're still thinking. Of something. If you weren't, you wouldn't just be brain-dead but clinically, comprehensively, in the ground six foot under, dead or in a coma.

I am, therefore, I think.

The following exercise may help convince sceptics

For the next 3 minutes, jot down all the thoughts that come into your mind. What you are doing is introspecting. You could call this free association because there'll be some links or associations between your various thoughts.

If you had no thoughts at all, worry.

Our minds, when we're awake, are nearly always busy. Thoughts flow along. The nineteenth-century American psychologist William James compared consciousness to a river and coined the famous phrase 'stream of consciousness'.

To empty your mind, you have to meditate. This is so alien to our normal manner of thinking that individuals who want to meditate have to learn special exercises. Many religions like Buddhism offer rigorous training in meditation.

So try a second exercise – and this one is much harder.

Imagine you're a baby

Put yourself inside the mind of a baby, an 8-month-old toddler who is crawling around his playpen. What do objects look like if you're observing them from a different height? How can you think of objects when you have no words for them because you haven't yet learned how to speak?

You've now grown up very fast and are 3 years old. You're going to kindergarten and you're pretending to be an astronaut or a doctor. Trying to imagine this is easier because you can use language but how do the world, your parents, other children look?

By comparison, trying to think like a 9-year-old or a teenager is much easier. Most of us have reasonable memories of significant events that have taken place after we're 8 years old. Hundreds of books and films depend on authors evoking their childhood. Many people have more fragmented memories of earlier events in their lives; I remember flying from Israel to Amsterdam and being offered chicken to eat on the plane.

But hardly anyone remembers anything of their life as a baby. A study in 1896 showed that most people's first memories were of an isolated event when they were three (Henri and Binet 1896). In films or ads when babies act sophisticated and speak, it's funny because it's impossible and outlandish. We know babies can't speak and can't possibly have the kind of thoughts they express in some TV ads or in the John Travolta movie *Look Who's Talking*. We're projecting an adult mind on to that of a baby or a toddler.

How do we get from helpless baby to knowing, ironic teenager?

In this book I look at different theories and aspects of cognitive development. Psychologists have tried to understand the stages by which children's thinking develops; some have also tried to understand the fundamental causes of development and have argued over whether our intelligence is a matter of **nature** or **nurture**.

Is cognition very much a matter of learning and environment or is it a matter of heredity? Is your fate sealed before you're born by your DNA and your genes or does everything depend on how you're brought up and the environment you develop in? **Nature theories** – also known as innatist, biological or the genetic position – claim heredity is far more important than environment. **Nurture theories** claim the opposite. The family environment, social class, individual experiences, the rewards and punishments a child experiences, determine her or his development. As we shall see, after a century of controversy it is possible to get closer than ever before to useful answers.

The twenty-first-century child

My aims in this book are, first, to examine the key research in cognitive development in a way that is accessible to those who love and live and work with children – parents, teachers, doctors, nurses, social workers, child carers and students of developmental psychology. Many parents want to understand the latest ideas in cognitive development – and many professionals need to in order to be effective. Second, I want to suggest that child psychology should take into account important changes in the way children grow up, changes that have an impact on their cognitive development. Children do not develop in a vacuum or the psychology lab. A leading child psychologist Tom Bower (1989) wrote of the changes he had seen in 'the theory of the baby'. In 1971, when he became a father, babies were seen as passive. In Scotland he couldn't buy slings or strollers that would allow a baby to sit up and watch what was going on. There were few audio-visual toys – certainly not interactive infant mobiles which, even if they don't yet exist, will soon allow an infant to have an e-mail address from birth. Bower wrote 'The market expected babies to lie back on their backs . . . contemplating a distant patch of ceiling or an even more distant patch of sky.' Today there's a huge industry catering for the active baby who can 'sit up in a well designed chair, able to inspect what is going on, able to look at a variety of mobiles and other toys.' (1989, p. 154).

We assume children are growing up quicker than ever before. Once 10-year-olds were really children. Now by that age they are often well on the way to putting aside childish things. They read fanzines; pre-teen magazines carry articles on relationships and sex; television programmes expose children not just to more violence but also to more issues than ever before.

Cognitive development is also becoming politically relevant. In Britain, the government has committed itself to testing children five times from the day they enter school to when they take exams: at 5 for a baseline assessment, at 7, at 11, at 12 and at 14. The European Community has decreed that children all over Europe are to be taught – and tested on – what being a citizen of Europe means from the age of 6.

The classic texts in child psychology – especially those of the great Swiss psychologist, Jean Piaget (1896–1980) – come from a time when education was more formal, when there was less competition, when children's TV didn't exist, when there was no Internet and when no commercial genius had dreamed of the idea of marketing to children and using focus groups of 6-year-old consumers. Even anodyne heroes like Babar and Winnie the Pooh appeared later (at least as major television and radio personalities) than Piaget's key books. The effect of exposure to the media on children's intellectual development is only now starting to infiltrate psychology. Students and parents need to be aware of these developments – and some of the relevant experimental work is hard to get hold of because it has been commissioned by advertising agencies. Glen Smith, director of the Children's Research Unit in London, a non-profit-making organisation that regularly studies children's attitudes, told me for an article I wrote on how children understand advertising, that it was not possible for some data to be published because his clients felt they needed to keep it confidential for commercial reasons.

As important as the cascades or deluges of information are changes in the structure of the family. Fathers are becoming more involved with children than ever before. A Prime Minister who admitted to changing the nappies – Tony Blair's proud boast – in the 1950s and even 1960s would have been seen as very peculiar. In 2000, on the other hand, Tony Blair insisted after the birth of his son Leo that he as well as his wife was having sleepless nights because the baby had to be looked after. Many children have to cope with divorce and with living in step-families which can make them more emotionally agile, and fragile, than ever before. It is not unusual for a 5-year-old child to be in a family that includes a new baby by her blood mother and a new man, an older sibling who was born to her blood parents and step siblings whose blood parents are her mother's new partner and his ex-wife. The Oedipus Complex for stepfamilies is an interesting subject. Inevitably, such social changes affect both the emotional and intellectual development of children. Cutting and Dunn (1999) report a study on 128 south London children which supports the idea that class and family experiences influence the way children develop an understanding of emotional language.

Child psychology cannot afford to ignore these changes if we are to understand the developmental pattern. Further, in the West, we should be sensitive to issues like poverty. It has been estimated that 5 million children die of malnutrition every year; millions more survive but suffer profound intellectual and emotional consequences. All our theories tend to be about how well-fed children develop but developmental psychologists in the West pay too little attention at present to poverty and malnutrition making – or breaking – the mind of a child.

I am writing at a time when some psychologists are questioning what is perhaps the most basic assumption underlying cognitive development – that children grow through a series of stages which can be meticulously identified. In his book *Emerging Minds*, the American psychologist Siegler (1996) claimed that we should stop seeing child development as a series of steps the infant climbs up and see it more in terms of overlapping waves. Siegler's ideas are in the process of generating considerable work and they do conflict with the classic theories of Piaget and his followers. The debate is one to return to at various points in the book.

Many of the arguments in this book cannot be conclusive because there are many enduring mysteries about cognitive development. What we don't know can be as interesting as what we do know – and what we don't know changes all the time in a swiftly changing world.

Contents

You can't understand cognitive development without understanding the brain. Chapter 1 gives a basic introduction to the cortex and how it develops from before birth to the teens. It covers the techniques used to study the brain and the methods psychologists resort to when studying babies who can't speak a word. The chapter also looks at the idea that the brain is a computer.

Chapter 2 looks at the work of Jean Piaget, the most influential child psychologist of the twentieth century, and argues he was extremely brilliant but had some curious emphases.

Chapter 3 looks at other theories of child development, including those of the Russian psychologist Lev Vygotsky who had the misfortune to upset Stalin. Vygotsky argued parents and teachers had an important part to play in helping children learn.

Chapter 4 looks at the question of moral development. How do children develop ideas of what is right and what is wrong and is that related to their cognitive development? The law in Britain, America and most European countries often assumes that children under 10 cannot tell right from wrong. Is that any longer realistic?

Chapter 5 looks at how children think about feelings, beliefs and other people. It is now clear that how children develop what philosophers call 'theories of other minds' is a crucial aspect of cognitive development – and some of the most persuasive evidence that children are growing up faster comes from these studies. If children are becoming more aware and more psychologically mature, in the West at least, should we not be trying to understand why?

Chapter 6 looks at the development of memory, an area which has seen psychologists at their most inventive. How can you tell whether a 3-month-old baby remembers anything since he or she can't yet speak?

Chapter 7 looks at intelligence testing and other ways of measuring cognitive development. IQ tests at best only measure a small part of it.

Chapter 8 looks at the nurture and nature debate in more detail. It examines not just the traditional area of intelligence but also that of personality. It suggests that we are on the way to finding a resolution of it.

Chapter 9 looks at issues of cognitive development in the classroom. It covers recent work on how children learn basic skills like reading and writing. Recently a bitter controversy has erupted between psychologists who believe that ability to produce and recognise rhymes is the best predictor of reading ability and those who differ. The chapter also deals with how we learn arithmetic and learning skills.

Chapter 10 looks at the influence of television and computers on the way children's thought develops – and raises the question of whether children seem to be getting smarter – and even perhaps getting smarter because they watch more television and talk about it.

Many chapters carry exercises in introspection and self-observation as well as what I call Parental Exercises. The great behaviourist John B. Watson made all his students in the 1920s fill out a Balance Sheet of the Self because he argued that psychologists could not practise on other people till they understood their own strengths and weaknesses. That is evidently true for psychologists and for all those who deal professionally with children. Parents aren't going to lose either if they are as aware as they can be of their own strengths and weaknesses.

1

The developing brain

Introduction

Agatha Christie's detective Hercule Poirot boasted his superior brain
let him solve murders that baffled Scotland Yard, so he was always
careful to keep his little grey cells warm. Cold might damage
brainpower. Marginally less eccentric, P.G.Wodehouse's clever butler
Jeeves believed eating fish kept his brain at peak power.

Outside fiction, it's proved more difficult to pin-point just what it
is about a person's brain that gives them remarkable gifts. Do brainy
people have a larger brain? Or a different balance of chemicals in the
brain? Pathologists have examined the brains of Einstein and Mozart.
Neither was radically unusual. Given the astonishing work they
produced – Einstein's theory of relativity and Mozart's wondrous music
– their brains seemed to be surprisingly like ordinary people's.

Ironically, the more we know about the brain, the more we realise
how little we know about how our ability to think develops. The
questions have become even more complex as some scientists like
Tooby and Cosmides (1998) argue that brain structures have possibly
changed more in the last million years than conventional accounts
allow. Evolution, they say, has affected the brain; human beings have
not just developed through 'culture'. The brain remains an organ
wrapped in awesome mysteries. The way the child's mind develops
is, obviously, rooted in how the brain itself develops, so it is useful to
have an understanding of how the brain works.

This chapter provides:

- **a simple guide to the way the brain develops from birth to adulthood**
- **descriptions of methods used to study the brain**
- **a guide to the many unsolved puzzles about the way children's brains develop**
- **a guide to the methods used in studying children**
- **an introduction to the nature *v* nurture debate. Is cognitive development the result of heredity and genetics or the result of environment? Or the result of both?**

Non-verbal subjects

When the brain is developing most dramatically – in the uterus and then in the first year of life – babies can't speak.

Let's say you want to find out if adults can spot the difference between triangles and circles projected for nanoseconds. You might tell your subjects to press the Red Button when they see a triangle and the Green Button when they see a circle. You can't begin to do this experiment if your participants can't understand the words Red, Green, Circle or Triangle. That's precisely the situation facing psychologists when they study babies. To overcome the problem, psychologists have devised a number of non-verbal methods. These include:

- following the eye movements of babies – we assume a baby is paying attention or concentrating on the people or things it is looking at;
- providing babies with 'unexpected' events – and seeing how they react;
- using trick environments like the visual cliff devised by the American psychologists Gibson and Walk (1960). They wanted to know if babies had any depth vision. They built a glass floor and babies were set to crawl on it. For the first few feet, the glass was right on top of a real floor so, if babies could understand what they were seeing, they must have realised they were crawling on something solid. After some feet, the floor beneath the glass fell away. The babies came to

what looked like the edge of a cliff. Did they stop or continue to crawl? Gibson and Walk reasoned that if they stopped babies had depth perception and some awareness of danger.

Psychologists have to be inventive when thinking of ways to study infants: in this cleverly designed visual cliff experiment, babies between 6.5 months and 12 months of age were reluctant to crawl over the 'cliff edge', suggesting they perceived the drop.

Other methods compare how much babies kick to different stimuli. All these methods are indirect and depend on interpreting the baby's behaviour.

The brain is mysterious so let's start with some self-observation.

Look at yourself in the mirror. Try to imagine what is going on inside your head. Write down or draw what you imagine.

There is no right or wrong answer to the exercise. What matters is that you realise the complexity of the brain. I sometimes imagine it like this. I think of a web of laser lights. Many colours, constant pulses of energy, new patterns that make and break and change. This isn't an accurate description because no one can really provide that yet, but it's a way of conjuring up images that address key aspects of the problem – the sheer computing power of the brain, and the connections between its cells.

And now, prepare to move from the poetic to the straight scientific.

The anatomy of the brain

The brain is an immensely complicated organ with over 100 billion brain cells or neurons, including glial and ganglia cells. The cortex, the top part of the brain, fits over the rest much like a teacosy covers a teapot. The cortex looks a little like a cauliflower. The brain has four **lobes** or, to continue the image, flaps of the teacosy. They are called: the temporal, frontal, occipital and parietal lobes. Each is named after the skull bone closest to it. These lobes are full of folds or convolutions as the cells are packed together tightly, under and over each other.

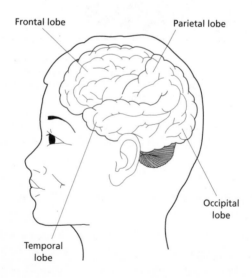

Frontal lobe   Parietal lobe

Occipital lobe

Temporal lobe

The lobes of the brain

The 'older' parts of the brain control basic functions like breathing and balance. All birds, mammals and reptiles also have a cortex but, as one goes up the evolutionary ladder from reptiles to dogs to apes to human beings, the size of the cortex increases. Allowing for the different body sizes of species, human beings have 3.2 times the cortex of the great apes. The most sophisticated chimpanzee – including a number of chimps trained by psychologists – can't master the skills that come naturally to an average 2-year-old.

The stages of brain growth

What follows requires some effort to grasp and the following key terms may seem daunting unless you have studied biology, but it's important to master them to get a sense of the structures of the brain.

Brain cell or neuron: the brain has many kinds of cell. Key brain cells are called neurons. They are either active or not, switched on or off. Messages pass electro-chemically (i.e. through electrical impulses or chemical messengers) from one cell to another. Brain cells form into pathways. Vision, hearing, speech all have their own pathways. It has been argued that when a particular memory is triggered and triggered again, the same pathway of cells becomes active. New thoughts almost certainly trigger new pathways or connections.

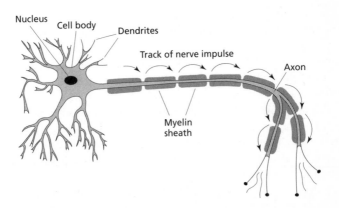

A brain cell or neuron: electrochemical 'messages' are received by the dendrites and transmitted along the axon from where they are passed on to surrounding neurons.

Axon: the long tube in a neuron that transmits information received by the dendrites to other neurons.

Dendrites: these are the long tentacles or branching part of the neurons at the end of the axon that receive messages from other cells.

Synapses or synaptic connections: when an impulse reaches the end of the axon of one neuron (cell A) it cannot leap straight to the dendrites or cell body of another cell (cell B). This is because the two cells are separated by a synapse. The word synapse is from the Greek for 'to clasp'. These synapses are tiny gaps just 200 nanometres wide between cells. Electrical impulses fire from cell A to cell B through chemical substances called **neurotransmitters**. In certain diseases like schizophrenia or Parkinson's, these neurotransmitters don't function properly so brain cells transmit messages too fast, too slowly or too chaotically. When you are conscious, millions of cells will be firing in your brain across synaptic gaps.

Myelination: cells are covered in a myelin sheath. This sheath allows information to pass more quickly down the cell body. Between birth and two years of age, the process of myelination proceeds at a dramatic pace.

Development of the brain

The brain starts to be identifiable when the foetus is 3 weeks old as a slab of cells in the upper part of the embryo. The brain and spinal cord roll into a hollow cylinder. In a few days, brain cells start to form and multiply around the central hollow; then, the brain cells move to the wall of the cylinder. This cylinder 'becomes' the brain during the 40 weeks in the uterus.

In the womb, the brain develops far more than other parts of the body. As a result, when babies are born, their heads are very large in relation to the rest of their bodies. Two-thirds of the brain is present at birth. In its structure and anatomy, the newborn baby's brain is remarkably like that of an adult.

Some psychologists suggest the brain is working in a quite sophisticated way even while the baby is still in the womb. Research in Ulster by Peter Hepper (1991) shows babies whose mothers listen to the *Neighbours* signature tune while carrying them can recognise those melodies very soon after they are born. The newborn babies kicked or moved to melodies they had heard while they were in the womb but did not respond to melodies they had never heard before. So, the foetus must in some ways have 'remembered' the melody.

At birth, the baby will have all its 100 billion neural cells in the brain. More brain cells do not sprout after the baby is born and becomes able to see, move and speak. Missing at birth, however, are most of the connections between the cells.

As the baby feels, moves and perceives, these connections are created. From the outset, heredity and environment interact. The baby's individual experiences create particular pathways and connections between particular cells. A baby brought up in a dark room does not form the pathways needed for normal vision for example.

'Making connections'

Films taken of brain cells connecting show the process as quite poetic. Little tentacles spread out from a cell and link up with tentacles from other cells forming an infinite web.

The diagram on page 13 shows some of the connections of one brain cell.

After birth, the dendrites develop spectacularly reaching out to make contact between brain cells. New synapses form. A good phrase to remember is 'synaptic exuberance' which researchers use to speak of the amazing multiplication of synapses after birth.

Again we are dealing with mind-boggling figures. Each neuron is estimated to have an average of 10,000 synapses or connections. Two brain cells will, therefore, have 1 million connections with other brain cells.

With already 100 billion cells in the brain that means there are 200,000 times more synapses in one person's brain than there are human beings on earth. It's hardly surprising we're individual.

Size matters

We have seen that human brains are larger than those of other animals. Until recently, psychologists played down the importance of the different sizes of human brains. Recent findings, however, suggest a strong link between intelligence and brain size and weight.

In *IQ and Human Intelligence*, Mackintosh (1999) points out that since 1990 studies of head circumference and IQ have all found a correlation between brain size and IQ. The average correlation was +0.38 which is not negligible. The samples in these studies haven't been small either; over 2,000 people had their heads measured.

Case history: how much of a brain do you need?

Another study, however, (Lorber 1981) shows how bizarre the brain can be. Lorber studied a number of Sheffield graduates who had mathematics degrees. Astonishingly he found that some of the graduates had large chunks of their cortex missing. Inside their skulls they had as much water as cortex but they behaved normally and did maths rather well.

There's also the famous nineteenth-century case of Phineas Gage. An explosion while blasting rock caused a crowbar weighing 13¼ pounds to transfix his skull and left frontal lobe. Not only did he survive but he remained able to perform all the tasks he had managed before. His personality changed, however. He became emotional, difficult and, yes, spiky and less en-gaging. He became very 'profane', apparently. Gage is not unique. In 1999, the American press reported a show business professional who shot himself in his mouth. Bullet fragments were splattered all over his frontal lobes but it didn't impair his ability to think. He still knows why he's depressed apparently!

Methods of studying brain development

The first two methods have been used for well over a century:

Studies of people with brain damage: if someone cannot speak properly and we discover their brain is damaged in a particular area, say the temporal lobe, then we infer the temporal lobe controls speech. Usually you couldn't pinpoint where the brain damage was until after someone had died.

Post-mortem studies: scientists have been able to carry out extensive research on brain development by studying the brains of foetuses, babies and young children who have died prematurely.

Both these methods have their limits. Studies of brain damage deal with individuals who have some kind of developmental abnormality or brain injury. In some areas such as language and autism, the study of such abnormal individuals has led to interesting insights. The nineteenth-century neurologist Broca was able to identify the third convolution of the temporal lobe as a key area for language on the basis of post-mortem studies; in the last ten years studies of autistic children have highlighted the importance of pretend play in normal development (Baron Cohen 1995). But it is not always clear how much one can deduce about normal brain functioning from studies of the abnormal. If someone without area X in the brain can't speak, it could be because area X is crucial in producing the ideas that produce speech, or in forming the intention to speak, or just because area X controls tongue movements or mouth movements.

Post-mortem studies have different problems. A normal baby develops quickly in the first few weeks of life. The only babies who die who are developing normally are those who die in road and other 'normal' accidents. (Children who die as a result of physical violence or neglect by their parents, for example, may be different.) And it is hardly surprising that parents often refuse to allow scientists to do research on their dead infants. Parents are living through a trauma.

Recent advances have led to three different methods of researching the brain so we can now see the brain inside and its activity while subjects are alive: *CAT scans* produce images of slices through the brain and show the layout of tissue. A beam of radiation passes through a patient's head to the detectors. Dense tissue absorbs more radiation than soft tissue. The patient is moved so the CAT scan can take images at many different angles building up a picture of the brain. *Magnetic Resonance Imaging (MRI)* involves putting the subject in a large magnet. The consumption of oxygen increases in active brain areas. Deoxygenated blood responds more to magnetism than blood containing a high level of oxygen so MRI makes it possible to map which areas of the brain are working very actively. *PET scans or positron emission tomography* where the patient inhales a gas or has an injection which contains a radioactive element and another chemical known as a radiopharmaceutical. This travels to the brain via the bloodstream and concentrates in the most active areas of the brain. It makes it possible to map which brain areas are being used because increased mental activity requires more blood flow.

All such studies have problems. If more blood flow indicates that area X is specially active while a baby plays with a mobile, say, what exactly does that prove about cognitive processing? Area X is involved

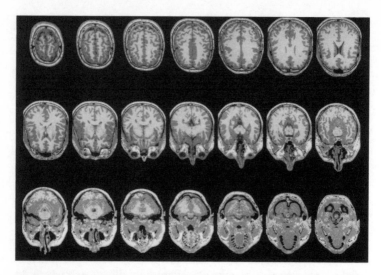

Measuring brain activity. MRI scanning creates 'slices' of the working brain. These scans are from top of the head (top left) to the jaw-line (lower right). Copyright © Wellcome Department of Cognitive Neurology/Science Photo Library.

but how? With babies there are also some more basic problems. Getting them to lie still may be a real problem. In addition, many intellectually exciting experiments are impossible to carry out for ethical reasons because these techniques expose the subjects to stress and radiation.

Key moments in development of the child and of the brain

To understand the brain science of cognitive development, one would ideally like to be able to flesh out a table as follows:

age	What is normal behaviour	What brain structures and pathways are formed
8 weeks		
12 weeks		
26 weeks		

The trouble is that it is hard to fill in the blanks.

First, the ages at which babies start to crawl, walk, speak and so on vary widely. All we can say is that something may be wrong if, by a certain age, the baby cannot do certain things.

The development of language is also very variable. Between the ages of 12 and 24 months, most babies start to show pre-linguistic behaviour. They point at objects. They babble. They start to use particular sounds, called 'proto words', for objects and people such as 'ta' for 'thank you'. But some babies don't start to do this till they are 30 months old. Some children don't produce words till they are nearly 4. Einstein claimed his parents fretted because he still was not speaking by that age. Proof that quiet toddlers are unusual but not necessarily slow.

If a child shows no speech at all by the age of 4, again, it would be reasonable to worry but children who are starting to speak just after their 1st birthday and children who say little till they are 3 years and 6 months old may both be quite normal. Instead of saying a particular behaviour normally appears at a particular age, many child psychologists choose to focus on certain landmarks in every child's history, landmarks that reveal a child's cognitive progress. These landmarks include the following.

- When the child realises each thing or person has a name. A psychologist writing at the start of the twentieth century, William Stern (1912), argued this was the main discovery the child makes. All cognitive development depends on that. Chimpanzees do not normally learn to point at objects; all infants do.
- When a baby realises he or she is a separate being.
- When an infant realises that reflection in a mirror is them.
- When children start to master language.
- When children start to pretend play. A child who imitates Superman has to be able somehow to grasp one or two key parts of Superman's identity, such as being able to fly and having a cape.
- When children get a sense that other people as well as themselves have a mind and feelings.
- When children understand human beings aren't immortal but must die – and that they too must one day die. In his book on baby and child care, Dr Benjamin Spock claimed that at the age of 4 children often start to ask questions about death – and where we go when we die.

These are all dramatic new cognitive skills that develop, very roughly, between the ages of 9 months and 5 years in normal children. There

Recognising yourself in the mirror: a developmental landmark.
Copyright © Sarah Wyld/Photofusion.

must be physiological changes or new connections in the brain that either cause them or reflect them. For example, is it only when the brain has X million connections running between area 21 and area 39 that the baby can look in the mirror and realise 'It's me'?

To be able to speak and pretend also must require dramatic changes in the child's brain. But we can't say there are areas of the brain which aren't working at 12 months when most infants don't speak and don't pretend and which then become active at 24 months when they can act out Batman. Being specific about the brain changes that accompany progress in development is very difficult. The problems become clear if you look at work comparing babies and monkeys.

Dramatic change

Fischer (1987) argued there were four periods before the age of 2 years when there were crucial brain changes that went together with dramatic changes in cognitive ability. Between the ages of *2 months and 4 months*, babies start to co-ordinate simple motor sequences so they can pick objects up. Between *7 and 8 months*, babies begin to master more complex action sequences such as pulling on a string to make a mobile move. Between *12 and 13 months*, babies manage complex sequences such as crawling to one end of a room, removing a toy from behind a cushion and giving it to a dog. This is intentional action. Intentional action is key because we tend to think a being has a real identity when he or she can will things to happen. The toddler becomes an agent, not a mass of responses. For philosophers 'agency' is a key concept. Then between *18 and 21 months*, babies start to speak.

Fischer claimed at each of these times there was an immense sprouting of synapses, of 'synaptic exuberance' as connections flowered in the brain. At 6 months of age, by comparison, there wasn't this surge of new connections.

The only data Fischer could offer, however, didn't come from human babies but from rhesus monkeys. The monkeys were trained to perform certain tasks and then 'sacrificed' and studied at post-mortem. Infant monkeys who could co-ordinate simple movements (Fischer's first period) and older monkeys who could co-ordinate complex sequences (Fischer's third period) did indeed show 'synaptic exuberance'. Monkeys who never mastered these skills showed no such growth of connections.

Fischer argued that in babies as well as monkeys there was 'synaptic exuberance' to match bursts in cognitive development. But his proof was indirect, assuming that what went on in monkeys went on in humans and he could offer no evidence for his fourth period since monkeys never learn to speak.

There is also evidence, Fischer claimed, for growth in head size which suggests growth in brain size. Between 7 and 8 months, head circumference grew by 2.7 per cent as against 0.1 per cent in month 9. Not everyone accepts Fischer's ideas, however and his problems in explaining how babies develop by studying rhesus monkeys high-lights the practical difficulties of developing convincing theories of human cognitive development. It is particularly telling that our information on a basic fact – how quickly children at different ages process information compared to adults – is far from comprehensive.

Neural changes

Janowsky and Carper (1996), in an article called 'Is there a Neural Basis for Cognitive Transitions?', focus on the shift in children's cognitive abilities between the ages of 5 and 7. They conclude there are important neural changes but admit they are diabolically difficult to specify. The best direct evidence they offer is a study showing that children who fail and children who succeed on a perceptual problem are using different areas of the brain to think at the time. Janowsky and Carper are very cautious in interpreting what this means.

They write: 'The infinite levels of the nervous system in which to search cause a burden of proof nightmare . . . does finding no relation between a behaviour and a hypothesised neural substrate mean that none exists? If no clear associations are found for a behaviour, it may mean that a further search at a different level of analysis is in order' (Janowsky and Carper 1996).

In other words, it's hard to find correlations between brain activity and behaviour but logically they must exist.

Critical periods

The best evidence for the behaviour change – brain change link in some ways comes from so-called critical periods during which the brain has to be exposed to certain experiences to develop new competences. The proper biological development of the brain, laid down in a child's genetic code, won't work if the child is deprived of run-of-the-mill experiences.

Language is probably the best example. If children do not hear language by the time they are 7 or 8 they will have missed the critical period for language and never learn to speak normally. It's as if the brain develops to a point where it has to absorb certain data. If it is denied that data, certain parts of the brain appear to atrophy.

Case history: wolf children

In 1798 a child who crouched on all fours was found in Aveyron France. Local legend had it the child had been brought up by wolves. A doctor Jean Marc Gaspard Itard (1774–1838) brought the child up and tried to train him to be human. He guessed the boy was 10 years old. He managed to teach the child to sit, to walk and to use a fork. He managed to teach him some words but the child never learned to speak properly – which rather broke Itard's heart. (There is incidentally a fine French film *The Wild Child* made by Francois Truffaut of how the wolf child was treated.)

In Agra, India in 1957 a hunter chasing a pack of wolves captured this 'wolf boy' running on all fours with the pack. The boy was identified as 'Pabsuram', now 6 years of age and taken from his family by wolves when he was only 18 months of age. During the years Pabsuram had been with the wolves he had developed the animal habits of a wolf, was unable to stand erect, emitted wolf-like cries and was unable to speak. Exposure to language enabled him to learn a few words. Copyright © Popperfoto.

continued

Another modern but equally remarkable case was that of two Bengali girls who were apparently brought up by wolves in the 1930s. The Rev A.L. Singh, a missionary, and his wife found the children and trained them. The Singhs kept a diary of their progress. When the children were discovered they had matted hair, lapped food from a pan and growled at anyone who came near them when they ate. Their sense of hearing was very sharp and they could smell meat from seventy yards. Neither child learned to walk upright. Kamala had learned about fifty words by the time she was 17 and became tame, a little like a good dog. The other girl died in her teens. The so-called Dogboy found in Chile in 2001 was not a real wild child. He had lived on the streets till he was six or seven and only started living in a cave with wild dogs.

Psychologists now think the reason these 'wolf' children failed to learn how to speak is they heard no speech during the critical period for the learning of language. The brain is 'wired' for infants to learn how to speak. As long as they hear language, the brain's 'wiring' will allow them to develop language. No one has to teach children; just overhearing language is enough. Once that critical period closes, months of speech therapy won't make the child speak normally.

Yet no one has identified what physiological processes in the brain switch on by 18 months to enable children to learn to speak. The individuals who solve that problem will deserve – and almost surely get – a Nobel Prize. There have been astonishing breakthroughs in brain science over the last fifty years and scientists are confident that more are on their way. Yet there are sceptics like Noam Chomsky, the great American linguist. In an interview Chomsky told me:

it may very well be that among the theories we are able to attain by our biological endowment there is included the theory of mind or it may be among the theories that we are not able to attain is included the theory of mind. In that case, it will appear that human beings have mystical, unintelligible properties because we as biological organisms will not have within our range (which is obviously a finite range) the theory which would, in fact, explain it. (1977)

In one sentence – the human brain will not be able to explain the human brain.

What kind of computer is the child?

Understanding the basic biology of the brain is also important because so many theories now use the image of the brain as a computer. There are also many studies that look at the speed of processing information as a key element in cognition. Salthouse (1998) looked at eight measures of cognitive functioning and compared the scores of subjects aged between 18 and 94. It was downhill all the time and Salthouse argued that a decrease in the speed of processing information was a major factor. Kail (1991) in a study of reaction times (in which the researcher studies how long it takes subjects to press a button when they see a triangle) looked at data from the ages of 3 to 15. He pooled the results of 72 studies and a total of 1,826 reaction times. He found in general that children's speed of processing increases as they grow up. That increase slows up as teenagers, around 13, begin to respond like adults. In the middle of a neat picture, Kail does report a peculiar lapse between 12 and 14 year olds. The 12-year-olds appear to be quicker than the older group.

It's clear either that this data is not very accurate or that something strange is going on. Why should 12-year-olds operate nearly at the speed of adults and 14-year-olds operate at roughly 70 per cent the speed of adults. Does puberty make the brain slow down? It's much more likely that these discrepancies are due to differences in the experimental groups. The 12-year-olds may have been smarter or doing better in school than the 14-year-olds. Kail could not control for such variables. The sum total of this research confirms common-sense observation. Children's mental processes speed up as they grow up but Kail does not have the data to pinpoint why. He has to remain unspecific in a way that is all too common when psychologists compare the brain to a computer.

The comparison between brain and computer is tempting, however, since they both are composed of many sub-units. Furthermore computers work in a binary language. (Binary means two). Every operation in a computer depends fundamentally on whether something is coded as 0 or 1. Neurons, we have seen, are either on or off so it's possible to say they are either in state 0 or state 1.

But the binary language of computers and the languages of the brain aren't exactly the same – and there are particular problems if we want to liken the child's brain to a computer. Let's imagine a conversation between a robot and its designer.

ROBOT: I know I was designed to help solve the problem of how to repair the Space Shuttle in space but I don't want to do it any more.

DESIGNER: Don't be daft.

ROBOT: I am not programmed to be daft. Space is boring. I want to play football and do poetry.

DESIGNER: You weren't designed to do that.

ROBOT: I've changed my mind

DESIGNER: You haven't got a mind to change. You're a computer. Your mind is what I designed.

This is sci-fi talk. Today's real computers couldn't change their minds or develop in this kind of way. Steven Spielberg's film *A.I.* highlights some of these issues.

Two of the most interesting commentators on the relationship between computers and the brain are the American philosopher Patricia Churchland and the neuroscientist Terry Sejenowski. They have argued (1994) that nervous systems are 'naturally evolved computers whose *modus operandi* (way of working) still eludes us'.

Part of the reason for the difference is the fact that computers are designed. Computer designers in 1955 knew what worked and didn't work in the computers of the early 1950s. They threw out what was obsolete and improved the design. The brain, Churchland and Sejenowski point out, has evolved differently. There hasn't been a succession of brain designers who have thrown out less effective models and replaced them with something better.

Without such constant redesigns, Churchland and Sejenowski argue, the brain is almost certain to have wired-in ways of performing tasks that are no longer ideal. There is little evidence the basic structure of the brain has changed since the Stone Age. In terms of evolution, 7,000 years is a tiny amount of time. But in terms of how we live and what we expect the brain to cope with, 7,000 years is a universe.

Stone Age humans lived in caves, had no electricity, didn't realise the earth orbited the sun, had no television and had not yet invented writing. Good ways of working for the brain in 10,000 BC may no longer be ideal but the anatomy of the brain hasn't changed since then. Many brain scientists argue we are still wired to 'fight and flee'. When our ancestors roamed the plains, they had a few essential needs. They had to eat, reproduce and avoid being caught and eaten by lions and other predators.

When our ancestors started to farm and to move to latitudes where there weren't lions, life changed. But it has all happened too quickly for the brain to change as well and as much.

Churchland and Sejenowski also argue the brain can't be compared to a general-purpose digital computer. Rather, the brain seems to be a linked set of highly specialised systems that do their jobs well but aren't that flexible.

A different view of the 'architecture' of the brain and its flexibility has been put forward throughout the 1990s by Tooby and Cosmides (1998). Their language is slightly less that of the computer though they also focus on specialised systems which they call **domain-specific modules**. Tooby and Cosmides attack what they call the Standard Social Science Model of development which sees learning and socialisation as the key processes in life. The model dismisses 'evolved biological or innate aspects – not just of human behaviour but of psychological organisation' as negligible. Our biology is infinitely adaptable. Give me a child till he is 7, declared the Jesuits and, later, John B. Watson, and I'll turn him or her into Francis of Assisi or Hannibal Lecter. The Standard model argues that 'to the extent that there may be complex biological textures to individual psychology, these are nevertheless organised and given form and direction by culture and do not import any substantial character or content to culture', Tooby and Cosmides (1998) state. Their critique argues the brain evolved not as a general-purpose computer but through the rough and tumble of life and even in the Stone Ages that involved more than 'fight and flee'. (If the ultimate goals of the brain are just the four Fs – feed, fight, flee and fuck – then no wonder culture is so important in shaping our highly modern behaviour.)

Tooby and Cosmides suggest we have different modules which result from our ancestors having to deal with different problems; these modules deal not with ultimate goals but embody what they call 'proximate calls'. In the course of evolution, human beings needed to recognise objects, outwit predators, identify plant foods, select mates, make tools, balance when walking, avoid snake bites, devise the most effective hunt-a-gazelle tactics and learn how to barbecue fish with a nice touch of herbs and many other skills. Tooby and Cosmides see each of these activities as a domain and each set of skills that allow such a set of behaviours as 'domain specific'.

This view allows them to offer an interesting solution to what they call 'the paradox of how to create a (brain) architecture that is at the same time both 'powerful and more general'. The answer is to put together ever larger numbers of specific mechanisms. Natural selection will have favoured brains which have more and more effective domain-specific modules. In the long essay that introduces their book they list over fifty such modules including a tool-use module, a theory-of-mind module, a face recognition module, an 'effort allocation and recalibration module', a friendship module, a sexual attraction module and so on. The more a system knows about the world and its characteristics, the more it can learn, the more it can solve. Tooby and Cosmides point out that William James argued humans have more instincts than animals not fewer.

Tooby and Cosmides' ideas are powerful and provocative but they are, in the end, just another model of brain development. There is another point that has to be remembered. If a computer had areas that were programmed to see and other areas to identify sounds, and the vision areas were destroyed, one could re-route the computer's sound programme so that it could take in visual information.

The brain just can't do this. There are examples of people who recover from brain damage to a surprising extent but there is evidence that certain areas are crucial for vision and certain areas for sound. You can't re-route the inputs for one area to another as you can in a machine.

Nature v. nurture: some history

For over 150 years scientists have argued about whether cognitive development is a matter of heredity or a matter of environment. Before there was a scientific psychology, philosophers claimed that babies were born a **tabula rasa** – a blank tablet. Babies learned everything from scratch.

One school of psychologists, the behaviourists (who believed one should only study observable behaviour), played down the influence of heredity. The founder of behaviourism, John B. Watson (1878–1957), who studied children extensively, argued that if he could

---

Lobster brains

Churchland and Sejenowski also warn against all too human arrogance. They offer an example which makes it only too clear how far we have to go before we can make the seductive comparison between the brain and the computer half way real.

The lobster's digestive system is controlled by a **stomatogastric ganglion** – ganglions are types of brain cell. The anatomy of these 28 cells has been mapped. We understand all the connections between them. But there is a mystery. The lobster's stomach digests in a clear rhythm. Despite intensive study, no single neuron or set of neurons has been found to be responsible for the lobster's digestive beat.

Trying to understand how the lobster digests is a problem that cannot be compared to the problem of how we are conscious or how we can do maths. If it's hard to compute how the humble lobster eats, it's not surprising that our theories of cognitive development remain a bit vague and unable as yet to pinpoint just what changes in the brain cause changes in the abilities of babies and infants.

The relationship of the brain and brain changes to cognitive development is also important in trying to understand one of the key controversies, that of nature *v.* nurture.

---

completely control any child's environment he could shape – or control – that child so that he or she would grow up to be either a pilot or an accountant or a gardener.

Other philosophers argued that babies were born with their fate already well determined. Before genes were discovered, philosophers like Descartes claimed the make up of a child's brain was largely sealed by their heredity. Those who held that view pointed to the fact that intelligent parents tended to have intelligent children.

Sir Francis Galton, a wonderfully eccentric Victorian scientist, wrote *Hereditary Genius* (1869) which traced the history of talented families. Galton found that 109 of 217 judges appointed to the High Court between 1660 and 1865 had relatives who were also eminent. Galton argued those judges who were appointed Lord Chancellor were probably the most able. Of 30 Lord Chancellors, 24 had relatives who were also extremely eminent.

Galton argued it wasn't the environment that made for this. It was a question of brainpower – and brainpower was inherited. J. B. Watson would have argued the reason the judges and their eminent relatives were all brainy was because they shared the same environment. The debate is still going strong though there are more facts about that than ever before as we shall see in Chapter 7.

Conclusion

I want to end this chapter on a note of caution. We've seen the brain is a complex organ that develops enormously in the womb and immediately after birth. We've also seen there are critical periods during which a child has to be exposed to some experiences for skills like language to develop. All this suggests the question of whether cognitive development is a matter of nature or nurture, the genes or the environment, is an immensely complicated problem. All too often, as we shall see, psychologists have not approached the issue scientifically. They've allowed their prejudices to get in the way.

Curiously, as we shall see in the next two chapters, the theories that have dominated cognitive development for most of the twentieth century have not been very interested in the specifics of brain development.

Thinking matter

We should never forget the complexity of the brain and that we still know little about how it develops.

The lobster research shows the real problems in trying to explain how a neurophysiological system operates as a whole – and, essentially, that remains the key challenge for the twenty-first century in explaining what causes or drives cognitive development.

Much research is limited by the fact that it has been done on animals.

Additional reading

Rita Carter (1999) *Mapping the Mind*. London: Phoenix.

2

The logical child: Piaget's theory of cognitive development

Introduction

Many psychologists believe Jean Piaget (1896–1980) was the greatest child psychologist of the twentieth century. When he died, the French newspaper *Le Monde* ran the news on the front page. In a tribute in *The Observer*, Oxford University psychologist Peter Bryant wrote 'child psychology would be a meagre thing without Piaget'. To his colleagues, Bryant said, Piaget was always – 'le patron', the boss.

Piaget's fame rests on his theory of child development. This mapped out the key four stages by which the baby becomes a savvy teenager who can do algebra, make fun of the Spice Girls and decide that her mother may be saying she's grounded tonight but she doesn't really mean it. From helpless baby to self-conscious ironic adolescent. Piaget also had enormous influence on education as his ideas suggested children had to learn at their own pace. He always made fun of pushy parents who devised programmes for getting young children to learn more, younger.

In this chapter we're going to look at:

- **the details of Piaget's theory of cognitive development**
- **critiques of his approach – including his neglect of social and emotional development**
- **experiments that suggest Piaget got some details wrong**
- **critiques of so-called 'stage' theories.**

Jean Piaget's theories still play a central role in the study of cognitive development. Reprinted from J.J. Ducret (1990), *Jean Piaget: Biographie et parcours intellectuel*. Lausanne, Switzerland: Editions Delachaux et Niestle.

Psychologists often claim their theories are pure, impersonal science but major theories tend to have roots in the lives of those who develop them. Piaget was a clever, precocious teenager and his experiences influenced his approach to psychology. Many critics feel he tended to over-emphasise the need for children to be logical.

The logical student

Piaget was born in the Swiss town Neufchatel on 9 August 1896. His father taught history at the local university and enjoyed discussing ideas with his son. Piaget went to school in the first decade of the twentieth century when it was normal to teach and be taught Greek, Latin and philosophy. He became familiar with the work of Greek philosophers like Plato and Aristotle. He was trained to handle **syllogisms**. Syllogisms can be compared to equations in mathematics; they state logically necessary relationships – and they can be expressed in mathematical notation.

Many people are terrified by formal logic – and it can be extremely complicated – but it needn't cause panic. A simple syllogism runs as follows:

If A is bigger than B

And B is bigger than C

A has to be bigger than C.

It doesn't matter whether A, B and C are cars, feathers, aeroplanes or Sumo wrestlers. The relationship is a necessary one.

Another syllogism runs:

All men are mortal

Socrates is a man

Therefore Socrates is. . . .

The answer is 'mortal' because, being a man, Socrates must share the characteristics of all men.

But some statements while put in the form of syllogisms don't hold true. For example:

All cats are mortal.

The Spice Girls are mortal.

Which of the following is true?

1. The Spice Girls are cats.

2. This is a trick question.

Given the information that cats and Spice Girls are both mortal, there's nothing else you can deduce about the Spice Girls or, indeed, cats. We know they die. That's it. So 2 is sort of right.

Piaget believed cognitive development was a long progression from infantile illogic – where you might believe the Spice Girls were cats – to logical maturity.

Exercise in self-observation

If you think about the things you think about – and the ways you think – you will soon realise that sometimes thinking is emotional or irrational or just plain weird.

Write down five situations in which you think logically.
   Then:
Write down five situations in which you think illogically or emotionally.

There are no right or wrong answers to this exercise. Its point is to get you to focus on the variety of your own thinking

Pondering ponds

Piaget's first subjects, however, were never known for their logic; they were molluscs. Piaget was fascinated by the question of how we know things, the problems and paradoxes of logic and of **epistemology**. But he was anything but an armchair philosopher. When he was just 11 years old, he spotted an albino sparrow in a park. Piaget sent a one-page article about this unusual bird to the local natural history magazine which duly published it.

Paul Godet, the curator of the Neufchatel natural history museum, invited the 11-year-old bird spotter to meet him. They became friends. Godet started to take the boy with him on walks to look at the wild life. Piaget became interested in pond life. Just as important as any facts of natural history Godet taught him, Piaget was learning the techniques of observing behaviour.

By the time he was 17, Piaget had published two papers on molluscs that lived in the ponds. One was in the weighty *Revue Suisse de Zoologie*, the leading Swiss zoology journal.

After he finished school, Piaget toyed with becoming a psychiatrist and went to study with Dr Eugene Bleuler, an authority on schizophrenia who ran a clinic in Zurich. In 1919, aged 23, Piaget abandoned this plan and went to the Sorbonne, the university of Paris founded in the twelfth century. There, Piaget met Theodore Simon who, with Alfred Binet, had helped devise some of the first intelligence tests. Binet and Simon studied what questions it was normal for children of a particular age to be able to answer.

At this point, Piaget had one of those Eureka-like insights. Instead of seeing at what age children could get the right answer to questions like:

What does 2 + 2 = ?

What will the sun inevitably do tomorrow?

Piaget asked what would happen if one got children to talk about these questions and tried to explain their mistakes. Piaget called this the 'clinical method'. He may have been influenced by his experience with psychiatric patients in Zurich who were encouraged to talk about their fantasies – and mistakes – as part of their treatment.

Piaget then returned to Geneva where he started to study toddlers at a nursery school, the Institut Jean Jacques Rousseau. People often assume Piaget first studied babies and progressed to study 3- and 4-year-olds. It was, in fact, the other way round. Piaget started on how toddlers think and some of his conclusions affected his approach to studying babies.

In 1925 Piaget married one of his pupils, Valentine Chatenay. Their first child Jacqueline was born later that year and Piaget immediately turned her into the first of his baby subjects. His three children – Jacqueline, Lucienne born in 1927 and Laurent born in 1931 – were all observed and studied. His theory of how babies develop is almost wholly based on his studies of his three children – and one needs to ask how typical they were. I met all three Piaget children in 1996 at a conference in Lisbon in honour of the centenary of his birth. Two of them were still living in the house they had lived in as babies where Piaget observed them.

Compare and contrast: the observer Piaget and the listener Freud

Years of observing animals had an impact on Piaget before he started to study children. A key difference between his theory and Freud's theory of **psychosexual development** is that Piaget based his ideas on what he saw children doing – and saying. He talked to 3-, 4- and 5-year-olds about their perceptions and ideas.

Freud, on the other hand, created a theory based entirely on what adults remembered of their childhood. Freud's main direct contact with a child patient was with a boy called Little Hans who was scared of horses. Even then Freud only talked to Little Hans once; most of the information was provided by Hans's father. Nevertheless, Freud decided Little Hans was frightened of horses because they had giant-sized phalluses and these provoked the child's castration anxiety! Whatever the flaws in Piaget's theory, he did study real children.

Yet both men produced stage theories in the end, theories which charted the child's development in terms of different stages through which they progress – in Freud's case, to sexual and emotional maturity, and in Piaget's case, to intellectual maturity. It has only been in the last twenty years that psychologists have started to ask whether such stages accurately reflect the way children develop. Piaget's theory, however, remains highly influential.

The four main stages of intellectual development

Between 1923 and 1936, Piaget observed his own children and continued to work at the Institut. As a result of his observations, he came to argue that between birth and 14 years of age, children went through four main stages. These are:

1. the sensory motor period
2. the pre-operational period
3. the period of concrete operations
4. the period of formal operations.

The names of three of these stages reflect Piaget's interest in logic and philosophy. **Formal operations** are logical operations such as being able to 'solve' syllogisms like the ones about Socrates and the Spice Girls.

Acquiring schemas

Piaget claimed intelligence stemmed from motor movements. As the baby starts to move itself and objects, it slowly acquires sensory motor

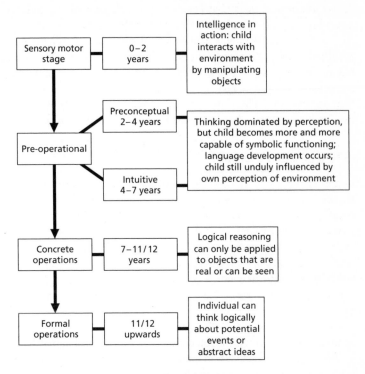

Piaget's four stages of cognitive development.

co-ordination and then **schemas**. A schema is a design or a mental representation. Piaget used two concepts to explain the development of these schemas – **assimilation** and **accommodation**. The terms need definition.

Assimilation, we assimilate information all the time. Sounds, sights, smells, touch sensations deluge us moment by moment. We take in or assimilate this bombardment of information from the moment we're born. But the brain can only cope with this flood of information by filtering some of it out.

Accommodation is more than the process of filtering which is key in perceptual psychology. For Piaget, accommodation occurs when 'the environment acts on the organism' and, as a result, the organism has to re-adjust and re-organise itself.

To give an example; a baby touches a ring suspended above its cot. The baby makes the ring swing back and forth, then holds it and sucks it. The child's ideas or schemas about grasping, seeing, touching are modified by these new experiences; the baby learns this particular ring belongs to the class of objects that also can be sucked and touched. The baby also learns that, in general, ring-like objects feel and taste different from bottles, say. The sight and feel of the ring are assimilated and that leads to a change or accommodation of the concept of rings.

Qualitatively different thinking

Infants have to learn first to co-ordinate their perceptions and movements (the sensory motor stage). Second, children between roughly 2 and 7 years of age have to struggle with wholly illogical ideas of the world when they can't even conceive what logical operations might be (the pre-operational period). Third, children from roughly 7 years to 11 years of age start to handle their immediate experiences logically (the stage of concrete operations). As long as they are dealing with something in front of them, concretely in the here and now, they can be logical.

Finally, round about 12, the child has sufficient experience and his or her brain has matured enough to become a truly logical human being.

The ways in which the child thinks at each stage are entirely different from those of another stage. Each stage of development has different attitudes, strategies and, indeed, dilemmas. Piaget talked of each as a **structure d'ensemble**, which is French for a whole, unified structure. Each stage also had a set of sub-stages.

Stages are not fixed but their sequence is

Different children develop at different speeds. Piaget never believed there was a fixed time for each stage. It wasn't a question of a baby aged 23 weeks having to be in sub-stage 3, paragraph 4 of the sensory motor stage. But Piaget did claim the stages and sub-stages followed one another in a fixed, inevitable pattern. No child, however brilliant, could leap from sub-stage 3 to sub-stage 7, skipping sub-stages 4, 5 and 6.

One of Piaget's key concepts was **décalage**: a French term which means slippage. In his later works, Piaget argued that children were not totally stuck in one stage. A child near the end of the pre-operational period, for example, might show some of the skills of concrete operations.

The sensory motor stage: roughly from birth to 2 years of age

Piaget often compared babies to primitive savages; the newborn was all confusion. At birth, a baby didn't even have that most basic aware-ness, the awareness of being a separate creature, the awareness that 'I' exist. Piaget wrote 'the baby is submerged in a chaos of interesting impressions without there being any distinction between his internal state and things outside' (1952).

He also wrote the baby 'looks at his own body the way we look at a strange animal'. When I will my hand to move to pick up that tasty apple, I know my hand is linked to my body and I can anticipate the apple's crunchy taste. I also know I have a separate body and that, at the end of my toes, the rest of the world begins.

The newborn doesn't realise, Piaget claims, his hand is part of his body – let alone that he can will the hand to move. The baby doesn't connect the image of her hand with the movements she sees. The baby doesn't realise there are boundaries between that body and the outside world.

Observations of children

When Piaget started, with his wife's help, to observe their children he quickly saw the progress the children made. I want to quote some of their first observations because they show Piaget and his wife were meticulous observers.

When Jacqueline was 2 weeks old, Piaget found that if he placed his finger against her cheek, she turned her head and opened her little mouth as if to take the nipple.

At 23 days Laurent would search for the nipple with his mouth. If it touched his right cheek, he would turn to the right to look for the nipple.

Piaget reckoned both these actions, the first signs of searching, were 'searchings which prolong reflex activity and which are as yet devoid of intention'. The baby didn't will them but they were still the first step on the road to intentional and intelligent behaviour. By the time they were 3 months old, Piaget's babies were far more active and co-ordinated. They would react to noises by turning in the right direction. They would look at objects. They would begin to reach out for them. These motor movements were the origins of intelligence.

The truth about objects

Piaget claimed that, for a baby, an object is not what an object is for the rest of us. If you see a table and the removal men put it next door, you assume the table still exists even though you don't see it. Babies, however, are completely at the mercy of their immediate perceptions.

The moment Laurent did not see his bottle, he acted as if the bottle did not exist. Out of sight was not just out of mind but totally out of existence. Piaget used his considerable ingenuity to confirm this finding which went so much against common sense.

Piaget knew that if a 12-month-old toddler is playing with a ball and an adult hides it, the toddler will try to find the ball. The toddler knows the ball exists even when he is not seeing it. Six-month-old babies, however, behaved very differently; they did not seem to realise objects were permanent.

Object permanence

Object permanence is one of Piaget's key ideas. Piaget hid objects. Sometimes the baby saw where Piaget was hiding them; sometimes the baby didn't. It didn't matter. Once the toy or ball disappeared, the baby behaved as if it had never existed. This was even true when Piaget just draped a cloth over a toy while the baby was looking.

Piaget reported that at this stage 'the child does not try to pull aside a cloth which has been draped over an object which is desired . . . the child acts as if the object were reabsorbed into the cloth' (1950, p. 132).

The next stage was also strange. Piaget studied a 10-month-old baby. Piaget rolled a ball behind cushions. The 10-months-old baby was more 'sensible' than the 6-month-old and did often look for the ball. But the 10-month-old looked in the wrong place. Instead of looking for the ball behind the cushion, Piaget often found these 'older' babies started searching where the ball had been before it disappeared.

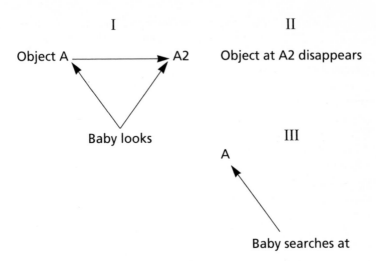

I

Object A ──────────▶ A2

Baby looks

II

Object at A2 disappears

III

A

Baby searches at

Ball disappears at location A but baby searches at location B.

Piaget was never known for his sense of humour but this research led him to crack one of his few jokes. He knew that babies often deliberately drop objects when they are 6 to 9 months old but he said that he didn't think it was because they were testing the laws of gravity. That was the joke. Piaget wrote when the cinema was very popular and he tried to give a feel for how the infant saw the world by comparing it to films. The infant sees the world 'as a slow motion film in which one tableau after another was presented but without fusion, without the continuous perception needed to make it comprehensible' (Piaget 1976).

A child learns to speak

What was crucial during the sensory motor period was feedback which allowed the child to develop schemas. At the end of the sensory motor period, the infant can walk, sit, get from one end of a room to another to grab a ball. The infant can identify his mother, father and siblings. He or she can often make all kinds of noises like 'goo' and 'mama' but a key ability is still missing – the ability to use symbols. For Piaget the question of **symbolic representation** was crucial.

Piaget distinguished between a symbol and a signal. Three red flags always mean 'shark is in the water . . . watch out'. This is a signal. A symbol is much more flexible. A picture of a table or the word 'table' can stand for many different kinds of table.

Babies first used sounds as signals. Some babies, when they were only 12 months old, would sometimes utter 'goo' when they saw their bottle. 'Goo,' Piaget argued, was just a signal – only used when the bottle was there. The baby did not say 'goo' when he wanted the bottle. To do that, the baby would need some representation of the bottle in his mind; so even when the bottle wasn't there, the baby could conjure up the idea of the bottle and say 'goo'. When 'goo' is a symbol it can stand for bottles that are present, bottles that I want, bottles I have enjoyed but have already drunk, bottles in all their variety.

As young children start to speak, a new world of ideas and concepts opens up for them. But Piaget claimed the child's language was very much determined by their logical limits.

The pre-operational period: roughly from the age of 2 to the age of 7

Piaget wrote 'the child's view of the world is always moulded on his immediate personal and sectional view' (1924). A 7-year-old child goes to school, can do sums and can tell his parents what he wants to do this weekend. But the 6-year-old also has relationships and can say why Harry, for example, is her friend. Many of Piaget's studies of children between the ages of 2 and 7 focus not on what you might expect – the child's development of language and of social skills – but, rather, on the ability to master complex thinking skills. His love of philosophy influenced him again. The name **pre-operational stage** reflects that interest in logic because the pre-operational child still cannot master real logical operations.

One of Piaget's sympathetic critics, the American psychologist John Flavell (1962) argued that Piaget was almost obsessed with what are called **reversible relationships**. A relationship is reversible when it is logically necessary. So, for example, 3 multiply 4 is logically bound to produce the same sum as 4 multiply 3.

But reversible relationships aren't just a matter of maths and logic. If Tim is the brother of Frank, Frank also has to be the brother of

Tim. If Chloe is the mother of David, David has to be Chloe's son. Between the ages of 2 and 7, Piaget claimed children still couldn't grasp these basic logical relationships and were also at the mercy of their immediate sensations and impressions. As a result, Piaget claimed pre-operational children were totally egocentric. He didn't use egocentric in quite the sense that we use it when we complain someone just thinks about themselves.

Pre-operational children were egocentric in that they were literally unable to perceive how anything might look from anyone else's perspective; they were always limited by the fact they could only hold in their minds what was in the here and now. Piaget sometimes called this **centration**.

Mountains, water, buttons: and pre-operational kids get them all wrong!

In one experiment, Piaget showed 4- to 6-year-old children a model of three mountains with distinctive features on their peaks. He also had a little doll. As the doll was moved about, the children were asked to pick which of a number of photographs represented what the doll was

The three mountains task. Piaget found that 4- to 6-year-olds cannot imagine what a view is like from anyone else's point of view or from anywhere else.

seeing. If the doll was on the highest mountain, she'd be looking down at the other mountains. If she was on the middle mountain, she'd be looking up at one mountain and down at another.

Piaget found 4- to 6-year-olds nearly always failed at this task. They couldn't imagine what the mountain view was like from anyone else's point of view or from anywhere else, they were perfectly egocentric.

Children failed on other tasks, too. Some of Piaget's most famous experiments were on conservation. He would show 4- to 6-year-old children Container A which was full of water to a certain level. In front of the children, Piaget would then pour the water out of Container A and into Container B. Typically, Container B was thinner and longer than Container A.

Piaget then asked the children if there was more or less or the same amount of water in Container B. Under the age of 7, children nearly always said there was more water in Container B even though they had seen with their own eyes it was the same water. For Piaget, this was proof again of the power of immediate perceptions. If Container B looks as if it has more water than Container A, the children can't remember what was in Container A and so say there is more water in Container B. They were victims of what he called *le figuratif abusif*, which can be translated as 'deceiving perception'.

It's sometimes tempting to see Piaget as the kind of man who'd have enjoyed playing tricks on children when he presented a kid's show on TV. In a third experiment, Piaget showed children a row of ten buttons. He then set out a second line of ten buttons. He would then remove one button but stretch the nine button line out so that it was as long as the line with ten buttons had been. Were there more or fewer buttons or was there the same number of buttons in this second line? Most children aged 6 would say there was the same number of buttons because the lines were the same length. Again their immediate perception made them behave illogically. Pre-operational children have not yet developed the schemas and the memory capacity to make the correct deductions. In real life, failure to grasp conservation leads to errors in estimating quantities and judging lengths.

If Piaget tested children aged about 7, they showed signs of being uneasy; this was typical of the end of each stage of cognitive development, but it was most pronounced at the border of concrete operations. As children got to 6 and 7, Piaget claimed they began to sense their view of the world wasn't quite in tune with reality, that it was wrong, primitive, illogical. They sensed what he called **disequilibrium**. Again it's tempting to see the influence of the time Piaget spent in the mental hospitals of Zurich. In their lucid moments, schizophrenic and manic depressive patients know they're not quite right and feel distressed by this failure.

The 6- and 7-year-olds were on the threshold of being finally cured of some of their logical imperfections.

Concrete operations (ages 7 to 11)

The phrase concrete operations is almost a pun on formal logical operations. Around the age of 7, children start to be able to handle concrete operations. They can master some basics of logic as long as they are dealing with the here and now and the practical. Flavell (1962) suggested Piaget saw these older children as being much more systematic in their cognitive behaviour.

A tale of eight bottles

One of Piaget's studies nicely illustrates the difference between the pre-operational and the concrete child. Seven-year-old children were given four bottles which contained different liquids. Bottle 1 contained a catalyst, a liquid which provokes chemical reactions and changes; bottle 2 contained water; bottle 3 contained oxygenated water; bottle 4 contained yet another catalyst. Children were given a fifth bottle labelled G and a pipette.

The children were then shown two more bottles. Bottle 6 contained a mixture of the stuff in bottles 1 and 3. Bottle 7 had water in it just like Bottle 2. Children then saw that if the liquid in bottle 5, the 'G' bottle, was mixed with the liquid in bottle 6 the mixture turned yellow. They also saw that if 'G' was added to bottle 7 this didn't happen. The liquid stayed colourless.

In other words $1 + 3 + G =$ yellow;

$7 + G =$ colourless.

The children were told to reproduce the yellow.

A 7-year-old boy Piaget saw as typical went about the task as follows. The boy started by adding a drop of G to each bottle. But that didn't turn the liquid yellow. The transformation required the child to pour the liquids from bottle 1 and bottle 3 together. A logical teenager (at least as Piaget saw this paragon) would immediately think it's now time to start a second systematic strategy and try $1 + 2 + G$ and, then would try, $1 + 3 + G$ and work methodically on. In contrast, the poor 7-year-old became depressed when he didn't get it right at once.

Failure made the 7-year-old erratic and, in a confused huff, the boy just poured one liquid into one bottle and then into another in a chaotic way. Soon the 7-year-old gave up.

Piaget argued this typical 7-year-old, just into concrete operations, had some of the right logical instincts. The boy knew what he was being asked to do and he had the bones of a strategy. When it didn't work out, however, he had insufficient logical skills and resilience to cope. He couldn't see the problem through systematically.

Formal operations (age 12 upwards)

The crucial progress the child makes between the concrete and formal stages is again a question of logical skill. Piaget gave the example of a 13-year-old called Cha. Cha was in the period of formal operations and the eight bottles didn't confuse him. Faced with the bottle and yellow liquid problem, Cha set out methodically. He started off by saying one must try the technique of adding G to each of the bottles. When that didn't produce the yellow, Cha said one must mix stuff from bottles $1 + 2$ with G, then if that didn't work out one should try $1 + 3 + G$ and logically on until one got the yellow liquid.

Even when he got it right, Cha wasn't satisfied. He thought there might be other answers, other ways of producing yellow. When the wily psychologist tried to persuade Cha that bottle 4 was full of water, Cha challenged him. Cha knew water is not a catalyst and so can't precipitate chemical reactions.

Cha's behaviour allowed Piaget to claim the 'formal' adolescent is no longer stuck with the here and now but can manipulate a large set of possibilities. The teenager is a logical maestro who can waltz with syllogisms and juggle abstract concepts. You sometimes get the feeling Piaget's ideal teenager spent his or her days thumbing through Socrates and Aristotle, singing syllogisms.

Piaget developed his stage theory in the 1920s but he never changed his mind about its basic truth. In 1976, Piaget sniped; 'Many authors currently criticise the idea of stages . . . But what seems to be essential, and I have been repeating it for years, are not chronological ages but the necessary succession of stages. One must have passed through each stage to reach the next' (Piaget, 1976).

Critiques

From 1930 to the early 1970s, there were surprisingly few critiques of Piaget. Since then there have been two kinds of attack. First, in the 1970s, a number of experiments suggested Piaget's theory was, if not wrong, not as right as everyone had believed. Second, some theorists like Howard Gardner of Harvard University argued against stage theories in general and claimed different cognitive skills develop at different – and unrelated – speeds.

But Gardner is not the only psychologist to wonder about stages. Flavell (1971) noted that children, according to such theories, seem to spend most of their time *being* rather than *becoming*. Yet childhood is about becoming, because all learning is a kind of becoming. By the time I have learned my 12 times tables and that Paris is the capital of France, I become a slightly different child. When I learn that my friend Fred may tell me lies, I become a very different child.

In a book which has received far less attention than Gardner's work, Robert Siegler starts from the point that 'my children have never looked much like those described in most theories of cognitive development'. He adds that he does not mean that they are 'deviant' or perform abnormally on classic tests but he stresses that their thinking is far more variable. If they are asked to perform a simple memory task, they might use very different strategies each time (Siegler 1996). Siegler amasses much evidence that shows that children use different strategies, which suggest very different levels of cognitive development, when doing the same task. A study of children who were confronted with a series of problems to solve showed that the best predictor of who got the most correct answers was the sheer variability of the strategies they used. Not all the strategies they tried were useful but it was a case of 'the more the merrier'. Siegler is a little sceptical himself of a model of cognitive development which reminds him of brainstorming sessions because, as an academic, he has been at too many 'get the brain juices flowing' meetings. But the young child seems instinctively to use many different strategies to tackle a new skill – say learning to speak – before focusing down on the right one. One should speak less of stages and more of overlapping waves, Siegler suggests, if we want to understand how children think, and how their thinking changes.

Siegler suggests that one reason psychologists have stressed stages is because they still believe in essences. What is the essence of the 5-year-old? Piaget's theory allows one to explain and describe it very clearly. As some of Siegler's studies deal with spelling and mathematics it's a subject we will return to in Chapter 9. One interesting point is that Piaget's theory developed from observing his own children and Siegler agrees that Piaget did at least notice there were periods when children did change and were highly variable; but Piaget believed this only happened at the point between two of the major stages – say between the sensory motor and the pre-operational stage. Siegler suggests changeable, erratic cognitive behaviour is far more common, and his book is a very useful summary of all the worries about stage theories.

There is also the question of how realistic Piaget's theory is. 'A theory of intellectual growth must take account of natural ways of thought, the ones that seem ordinary or intuitively obvious or lebensnah' argues Jerome Bruner (1972). *Lebensnah*, a useful German word, just means 'near to life'. And for Bruner, Piaget sometimes fails that test because of his emphasis on logic.

As criticism has developed, a number of sweeping criticisms have been made of Piaget's approach. These can be summarised as follows:

- Piaget over-emphasised the importance of logical thought and philosophy.
- Certain experiments suggest children didn't really understand what they were being asked to do. They failed because they got confused by unclear instructions.
- Piaget ignored the social and emotional development of children. Cognitive development is not just intellectual development.
- Piaget was hostile to the possibility children can be taught skills they don't yet have naturally. For him, the child has to mature. Yet there is evidence that children can be taught skills they don't have.
- The stages may under-estimate the extent to which children change all the time as they are growing up.

Parental exercises

One of the great pleasures of being a parent is of seeing your child grow up. Piaget was the great keeper of the diary of how his children's thinking grew. I feel very glad that because I was studying how laughter develops and my children were very much the main subjects of this experiment I have detailed notes of some of their behaviour from when they were tiny. The advent of video means that many people now assume they will take home-videos of their children. Obviously these are a way of keeping track of what your children do as they grow up. Enjoy the experience of recording them but don't feel tempted to push your kids. In this I think Piaget was totally right. The obsession with proving that your toddler is brighter than the toddler next door will only end in tears and, possibly worse, in neuroses. Filming your children should be fun and, as long as you can make it fun for you and your toddlers, you could film how they respond to the exercises below.

But if you find yourself caring about whether they get it right or wrong rather than just enjoying what they are doing, smack yourself.

Experiments that go against the theory

Balls and babies

Babies were allowed to watch a bright ball which was swinging back and forth like a pendulum (Bower 1973). The babies paid attention because their eye movements remained focused on the moving ball. Bower then put a screen in front of them so that for part of the swing of the ball it was obscured. Piaget would have predicted the babies would look nowhere in particular when the ball disappeared.

Bower found this did not happen, however. The babies did not peer randomly or look back to where the ball had disappeared. Rather, the babies kept on following the usual swing of the ball with their eyes. One could say that they seemed to be expecting it to re-appear from behind the screen just as it had done before. After Bower, a number of similar experiments (such as Baillargeon 1993) suggested that babies are surprised when objects appear or disappear in a way that is illogical.

Baillargeon found babies react with surprise – typically surprise is measured by the length of time the babies gaze at the object. This line of study claims that babies can only be surprised if they already have a sense of the permanence of objects.

Hughes: and the doll

Hughes replicated Piaget's three mountains experiments with dolls but using far simpler materials and a more realistic situation. He arranged three dolls as follows. One doll was a little boy; the other two were policemen. The child has to decide in which square to place the baby doll so that the policemen cannot see him. Hughes's argument is that only when a child can take the perspective of the other – i.e. the policemen – can he or she successfully conceal the doll.

Hughes found children aged as young as 3 years old could hide the doll in the one square the policemen could not look into – square C.

Hughes then extended the work by having three policemen and two new squares.

The task was now too complicated for 60 per cent of the 3-year-olds but 90 per cent of the 4-year-olds managed to get it right. They could

The two policemen version of Hughes's experiment. Children as young as 3 could hide the doll in the one square where the policemen could not see it – c.

see the one square where the boy could hide from the three prying policemen.

Hughes's work questions whether children are really as egocentric as Piaget suggested. His research suggests that even 4-year-old children can imagine how something will look from a different perspective.

Transitive inferences

Another powerful set of critical experiments was carried out by Peter Bryant who is, in general, an ardent supporter of Piaget. Bryant wanted to see if young children were unable to make logical deductions. He and his co-worker Trabasso constructed an ingenious machine which looked a bit like a xylophone. It consisted of 5 sticks of different lengths: A was 7 inches long; B, 6 inches; C, 5 inches; D, 4 inches and E, 3 inches long. Children were shown these sticks. Each stick was then placed in Bryant's contraption. It consisted of five holes drilled to different lengths so that the same length of stick, 2 inches, always projected.

Once the sticks were inserted, all the children could see protruding was 2 inches of any stick. All the protruding sticks were of identical length: 2 inches. Yet when Bryant and Trabasso asked 4-year-old children if A was bigger than D, they were able to answer the question correctly.

These children were not being mesmerised by their immediate perception – that the section of the sticks poking out was just 2 inches long. Bryant argued young children were capable of logical inferences – that A is bigger than D – if they were given some sort of help and if what they were being asked to do was clearly explained to them – in language they could understand.

You can never escape the syllogism

These experiments have themselves become controversial. It has been argued Bryant and Trabasso made the problem too easy because the only judgement children had to make was in the form of whether A was bigger than B, a comparison of two objects. Real transitive inferences, Andrews and Halford (1998) claim, require the ability to integrate three pieces of information rather like the premises of syllogisms.

If John is taller than Peter

And Peter is taller than Mary . . .

Yes, of course, John is taller than Mary but logical ability means mastering the three-part thought: 1. John is taller than Peter and 2. Peter is taller than Mary and 3. work out the position of all three in terms of height relative to each other.

Andrews and Halford got children to use blocks marked A to E to build towers and asked them to predict where block B would be in relation to block D and in relation to other blocks. The authors claim that only 20 per cent of four-year-olds manage to make transitive inferences involving comparing three blocks and that this success rate grows to 53 per cent of 5-year-olds and 57 per cent of 6-year-olds. But even these results suggest that a majority of children can think more logically than Piaget assumed before they reach the age of 7, the start of concrete operations.

Naughty conservers: experimenter effects

A fourth experiment also casts doubt on one of the key experiments in Piaget's theory – the conservation experiment. Why does who pours the water matter? McGarrigle and Donaldson (1975) introduced a naughty bear into the equation. The delinquent bear set about attacking the objects to be conserved. Then, instead of the high status adult pouring the water or altering the rows of sweets or buttons, it was left to the naughty bear to do it.

When the bear poured the water or shifted the buttons, children as young as 4 were able to produce the logical answer. They weren't fooled by the fact that one container looked different. If children can get the right answer in these circumstances, critics wonder if adult experimenters, who know what the result Piaget predicts is, betray the fact unconsciously. Children pick up these 'unconscious' cues and then regurgitate the answer Piaget's theory claims they should. Experimenter effects are common in psychology.

Neo-Piagetian theory

Followers of Piaget who came to realise his research needs updating are called *neo-Piagetians*. The most interesting development of this is the work of Robbie Case which is examined in Chapter 5.

Many critics suggest the real problem with Piaget's work is that he didn't really try out alternatives. One sign of being capable of formal operations is trying to weed out incorrect explanations by testing all possible alternatives. These critical studies suggest Piaget wasn't operating in the logically perfect manner he demanded of others. He blinded himself to possible alternative explanations for some of his results.

There are even more subversive facts. In a study of British undergraduates, Wason and Johnson Laird (1972) found most of them can't think logically in any case. In one study, they presented students with four cards marked on one side as follows:

A D 4 7

Students had to say which card needed to be turned over to confirm the proposition that if there is a vowel on one side, then there is an even number on the other. Ninety-two per cent of students contented themselves with turning over the card with the A on it. Only a truly logical 8 per cent realised that to confirm the hypothesis, one also had to see what was on the other side of the 7. That could also be a vowel, after all.

Many students turned over the A and were amazed to discover they had not solved the puzzle correctly. Cox and Griggs (1982) found similar results in America. Perhaps even more astonishingly, Golding (1979) found patients with particular kinds of brain damage often did better than the fine-brained students.

The problem may come down to Piaget's love of logic. Most of us are not as familiar with manipulating logical equations as he imagined. Wason and Johnson Laird repeated their experiment using envelopes. The hypothesis to be tested was: if an envelope is sealed it has a 5p stamp on it. To get that right, you need to look at the back of the 5p envelope and also at the back of the 4p envelope. With these realistic materials, 92 per cent of students got the right answer.

The conclusion has to be that many adults never achieve the holy grail of formal operations. Piatelli Palmerini, a well-known Piaget scholar, has studied what he calls 'cognitive illusions' and concluded that adults are constantly fooled by logical questions because we have 'tunnel vision', focusing all too easily on one aspect of a problem (1994). Piatelli Palmerini argues there are seven deadly cognitive sins which prevent us from being truly logical.

A more recent study by Bradmertz (1999) has followed up 62 children who were first studied when they were 7 years old. Bradmertz uses a set of tests which followers of Piaget now accept define formal thinking. Only one of the 62 children had by the age of 15 managed to reach the stage of formal thinking. A similar study by Precheur (1976) found that only 4 per cent of 18-year-olds who were studying humanities and 18 per cent of those who were studying experimental sciences reached the formal operations stage. Precheur did find that a majority of students of mathematics (60 per cent) were in the formal stage, however.

The results reported above are a little shocking. It seems unlikely that teenagers develop radically improved ways of thinking after 15 or 18. The link between mathematical ability and formal competence highlights many of the criticisms of Piaget. If it is only mathematicians who ever really master formal operations, where does that leave the rest of us? It is not wholly clear what the implications of these findings are. Does it mean that only the mathematically skilled ever become really intellectually mature? Or does it mean that many people can perform very well in all kinds of other disciplines – English, writing, art – without having reached the final stage Piaget identified as the pinnacle of cognitive development? Finally, where do such results leave psychologists? Many psychologists dread statistics and are not that mathematically competent. No one to my knowledge has yet tested psychologists to see whether as a profession we are fully mature intellectually. Probably not!

Conclusion

In real-life situations, young children have more cognitive sense than Piaget found in his experiments.

It is now over 75 years since Piaget started his research. We need to ask a further question. Was there always something wrong with his theory or have children changed between the late 1920s and today? As children are bombarded with information, watch endless TV programmes, play computer games and surf the web, one has to ask: are they growing up in the same way Piaget did, discussing Plato and observing molluscs in Neufchatel before the First World War? And if the life of the child and his, or her, culture are different, won't that affect how he or she thinks and learns to think?

Thinking matter

Always remember what aspects of cognitive development Piaget ignored. Bradmerz's results on formal operations emphasise Piaget was perhaps over-impressed by mathematical logic.

Ask whether the fact that Piaget did much of his experimental work 75 years ago is relevant. Have children changed over the twentieth century?

Consider the issue of stage theories. Does the evidence support children developing in global stages or do skills develop in more piecemeal ways?

Additional material

M. Boden (1979) *Piaget*, Fontana, remains an excellent introduction to his ideas.

M. Donaldson (1978) *Children's Minds*, Fontana, gives a rounded view of research that examines Piaget's ideas.

3

Egocentric or social animals? The work of Lev Vygotsky

Introduction

In the 1960s, Piaget read for the first time the work of a Russian psychologist Lev Semenovitch Vygotsky (1896–1934). Piaget said he was very sorry never to have been able to talk to him for Vygotsky's theories were an interesting contrast to his own. Vygotsky died in tragic circumstances in 1934 at the age of 38. That early death helped make Vygotsky an immensely romantic figure. In this chapter we're going to look at:

- **Vygotsky's ideas on thought and language**

- **Vygotsky's theory that children develop first as social beings – and then as cognitive ones**

- **Vygotsky's theory that egocentric speech isn't really egocentric**

- **Vygotsky on how children flourish when helped and the zone of proximal development.**

Like Piaget, Vygotsky was born in 1896. Again, I think it's important to understand something of Vygotsky's life to see what influenced his ideas.

Lev Vygotsky (1896–1934) emphasised that cognitive development depends very largely on social factors.

Vygotsky's career

Vygotsky was a Jew at a time when it was the official policy of the Tsar of all the Russias to persecute Jews. For Jews to study at a university was very difficult. In the 1890s, only the most brilliant Jewish students were admitted.

Vygotsky was an outstanding student and, normally, would have walked into Moscow University. He spoke English, French and German; he had a good knowledge of literature. But just when it was time for him to apply, the Tsar changed the rules. The Tsar feared too many of the best students were Jewish so he decided to set up a lottery for Jewish would-be students. With this enlightened reform, the Tsar hoped he'd now have as many stupid Jewish students as stupid Christian ones.

The brilliant young Vygotsky thought this new law ruined all his hopes but when the lottery results were announced, he was proved wrong. He won one of the places and went to Moscow University to study law.

In 1917, when Vygotsky was 21 years old, the Russian Revolution changed the country utterly. The Bolsheviks ousted the Tsar; the Communists took power.

Marxism

Today we see Communism, the political expression of Marxism, as a failed ideology, cruel and corrupt. In 1917, however, Communism offered hope of an equal world. It was idealistic, had huge intellectual energy behind it and attracted intelligent young people like Vygotsky.

Karl Marx (1818–83) was the inspiration for the Russian Revolution. Marx saw himself as a political prophet and a social scientist. He argued societies evolved through different stages – barbarism, feudalism, capitalism – and that capitalism was both unjust and inefficient. Though Marx never produced detailed psychological theories, he emphasised the role of social relations and power relations between people and different social classes. Human beings could only be understood in the context of their society.

Until 1917 Russian psychology, like most Western psychology, focused on the study of the individual rather than the group or the society. Piaget's theory emphasises how the baby reacts to objects rather than to people like his parents, siblings and playmates.

The young Russian psychologists took the opposite line after the 1917 Revolution. The key fact of Marxist psychology was that babies, children, all human beings were social animals. You had to study the individual in his or her social context to understand their development.

From 1924 to 1934, Vygotsky carried out research on children. His aim was to produce a 'genetic' psychology. He did not mean anything to do with genes or DNA but a psychology of development from womb to tomb. Vygotsky's infant wasn't egocentric or logical or illogical but social and communicative. Vygotsky was more of a theoretician than a careful experimenter and many of his writings are more brilliant sketches than they are fully developed research.

Stalinist Russia

After the death of Lenin in 1924, Stalin took control of the Communist Party. Stalin was dogmatic and a brutal dictator. Vygotsky did not always toe the party line and Stalin, much like the Tsar before him, was anti-Semitic. The brilliant young Jewish psychologist got into trouble with the authorities. Many of his papers were not published. Then, in the early 1930s, Vygotsky developed tuberculosis which killed him. The West knew little of his work till the early 1960s when there was a cultural 'thaw' and the Soviet authorities allowed some of his papers to be published. Vygotsky's ideas have become influential since then. Veresov (1999) provides a good history.

Exercise in self-observation

What do you think about most things or people?

Jot down your key thoughts for the next 5 minutes.

How many of these thoughts are abstract?

How many are about people?

How many seem to you to be about something else?

Tot up how many ideas you had fitted into each category. Some people find this kind of introspection dull. Other people find it interesting because they discover whether they are person- or object-oriented. It could be argued Piaget was object-oriented, Vygotsky person-oriented and this accounts for the differences in their theories.

The social child

Vygotsky had a number of key ideas. He argued that the child develops as a social creature from the start – and is not egocentric. The child's egocentric speech is not primitive but is produced as the child struggles to deal with abstract ideas. Eventually egocentric speech becomes inner speech – and most adults think using inner speech. Children have a 'zone of proximal development' often abbreviated to ZPD. This is a complicated term for a simple idea. Assume I can do task A but that task B is just too difficult. With help from other people, I can master task B. It's just beyond what I can do on my own but it is a task I can accomplish with help. The ZPD is the region between what a child can do unaided and what they are potentially capable of with a little help. In play, children create their own zone of proximal development because play stretches them – and especially stretches their imagination.

Play has always been an important factor in development. Copyright ©
Sophie Clausen.

Marxist Vygotsky and logical Piaget: the battle of the polite giants

Vygotsky wrote an introduction to the first of Piaget's books to be published in Russian. He praised Piaget's methods but argued the Swiss psychologist was often wrong. Vygotsky was heavily influenced by the work of Charlotte Buhler who studied the way babies and children started to speak.

For Piaget, language came out of the logic and cognitive development of the child. Only at the end of the sensory motor period, when the child becomes capable of **symbolic representation**, does he or she start to learn to think and speak like an adult.

Vygotsky argued the initial babblings of babies and young infants are neither symbolic nor immature attempts to represent anything. Rather, they're social and emotional signals. He compared these babblings to the cries of apes. Research in the 1920s had shown colonies of apes start to scream when they sense predators nearby. The apes' cries are expressions of fear. Their purpose is also to warn other apes of danger. Apes also utter cries when they greet other apes. These cries are not symbols but signals, used to express feelings rather than represent emotions.

Vygotsky suggested apes never learned to speak like humans do because they never advanced beyond using cries as emotional and group signals. This theory left Vygotsky a problem. It would have been nice to explain how our ancestors had developed these social cries into human languages that can handle complex concepts and abstract ideas. But Vygotsky said little about this – a weakness in his theory. But there's certainly plenty of evidence of how limited ape 'language' is.

Case history: trying to teach chimps how to speak

A number of psychologists have tried to teach chimps to speak or use American sign language. The results have been mainly disappointing. Nim Chimpsky (named after the linguist Noam Chomsky, for psychologists do fancy themselves as comedians) managed to learn two-word combinations such as 'Banana please' or 'red Triangle'. This is the speech of an 18-month to 24-month-old child.

There has been some excitement recently based on Sue Savage Rumbaugh's work with chimps who seem to teach their children some rudimentary sign language. No chimp, however, has produced three- or four-word utterances let alone the kind of sentence 3- or 4-year-olds scream as a matter of course in a playground such as 'I'm King Kong and bigger than you'. This suggests chimps cannot attach to signals or signs, the layers of meanings that are part of learning to speak. Itard's wild child also could not get to this point.

Vygotsky's view of language makes the young child the opposite of egocentric. His toddler is a social creature. His babbles because she feels happy to be with others or wants to draw their attention to something like the bottle or because she is afraid – and wants to convey that fear to others. Baby cries because he is dirty or wet and wants mummy or daddy to change his nappy.

Language as symbolic representation comes later. The key 'discovery' for the child is when she or he learns to point and realises every object has a name. Vygotsky called this the turning point and defined it as follows:

> Before the turning point the child does recognise a small number of words which substitute for objects, persons, actions or desires. At that age the child only knows words supplied by other people. Now the situation changes; the child feels the needs for words and actively tries to learn the signs attached to questions. (Vygotsky 1962)

Before the turning point, Vygotsky suggested, the child's language is pre-intellectual – just like a chimp's. There is intelligence but it is non-verbal. After the turning point, both thought and language begin to grapple with ideas and concepts.

Vygotsky suggested four major stages in the development of thought and language: a '*primitive*' stage when speech is pre-intellectual and intelligence is non-verbal; the stage of *practical intelligence*; the stage of *external symbolic representation*. So, for example, the child counts on his or her fingers or uses memory aids like picture cards to remember words. For decades, teachers tried to stop children counting on their fingers. Now, the wisdom is that it's a good idea precisely because it's recognised as a stage when children need external help to learn to handle symbols.

According to Vygotsky, children speak to themselves most when they're struggling to master symbolic representation. Egocentric speech is almost a learning aid or tactic.

The fourth stage comes when the child is mature enough not to need external symbolic aids. The child can now *internalise symbols*. A girl of 8 wouldn't have to speak a running commentary on her actions because she's used to silent inner speech. For Vygotsky, silent inner speech is vital. We need it to make plans, for example. If you can't say to yourself '**tomorrow**', what kind of future plans can you make?

Egocentric speech

Vygotsky accepted Piaget's observation that 3- and 4-year-olds are often egocentric in their speech but Vygotsky wondered why. He decided to examine how certain situations affected the amount of egocentric speech children produced.

Vygotsky was familiar with work done on apes where they were placed in a cage with a banana that was out of reach. Often there'd be a stick in the cage. It would take the apes hours to realise they could use the stick to get the banana down so that they could eat it (Köhler, 1925).

Vygotsky arranged a series of experiments in which 3-year-olds were placed in a similar situation. For one girl, Anya, aged 3 years 7 months old, what followed was instructive. Situation: a candy is on the cupboard. A stick is hanging on the wall. She reaches up. 'It's very high. I should call Lyuba so she can get it.' Anya tries again to reach the candy. She repeats that she can't get it because it's too high. She now grasps the stick but she doesn't use it. 'No way to get it, too high.' She reaches for the candy again but with her free hand, i.e. not the hand in which she holds the stick. She then complains her hand is tired. 'I am still small. I can't get it.' She swings the stick a few times and then stands on the chair. She laughs and now, still standing on her chair, swings the stick. 'Pah-pah,' she says and finally on the chair, swinging the stick, she gets the candy. 'See I got it with the stick. I'll hang it up at home and my cat will be reaching for it.' (Quoted in Valsiner 1984)

Vygotsky argued Anya spoke to herself, and produced egocentric speech, because she was trying to solve a problem. Her words certainly show thinking in progress. She's still too small to get the candy. Older children don't need to utter this stream of words because they can internalise speech. But Anya doesn't quite say what one might expect if egocentric speech is part of problem solving. She keeps on repeating that she can't get it, it's too high. No solution there! Even if the solution is non-verbal – suddenly seeing a pattern where she can use the stick to get the candy – she says nothing at the time she reaches it. She never speaks about the 'insight' of using the stick until long after it has happened unless 'Pah-pah' stands for Eureka which Vygotsky doesn't suggest.

So Vygotsky's own case doesn't quite confirm his theory.

Vygotsky also studied what happened if a child was placed in a situation like Anya's but in a room with a deaf child or with foreign children or when loud music was being played. Here his ideas worked

Children use inner speech to help steer themselves through unfamiliar tasks.
Copyright © Bob Watkins/Photofusion.

better. In all these instances, children produced far less egocentric speech. If the child knew there weren't any proper listeners, the child responded to that social reality and spoke less. This suggests the child is aware of the presence and capacities of others. A totally egocentric creature wouldn't be so sensitive.

Children speaking to themselves

A number of studies have attempted to verify Vygotsky's ideas on egocentric speech and especially his idea that children use it to help them deal with problems. Furrow (1984) compared the social and private utterances of 23- to 25-month-old children in the presence of an experimenter. Furrow evolved twelve different categories of speech including 'self-regulatory'. A self-regulatory utterance would be when the child would say 'careful . . . going too fast,' for instance.

Furrow looked at instances where children were talking to themselves. A large number of these utterances described what they were doing but a large number also included self-regulatory utterances. The child used speech to steer himself or herself. Furrow's findings partially confirm Vygotsky's ideas.

Bivens and Birk (1998) moved the research on. They observed older children aged from 6 years of age to 8 years of age. The children were working at maths problems. The researchers looked for three different kinds of verbal behaviour – first, irrelevant private speech such as comments to toys, to absent friends and word play, etc; second, task-related egocentric speech such as sounding out numbers aloud; third, external manifestations of inner speech, children muttering, lip and tongue movements, etc.

Task-irrelevant speech decreased with age while signs of inner speech increased. Again this suggests Vygotsky was on the right track but it still doesn't quite prove his thesis. Vygotsky was not claiming there was a correlation between egocentric speech and concentration and self-control but that the child achieved self-control first by ego-centric speech and later by driving egocentric speech inwards. Cause and effect aren't so easy to prove here but Vygotsky's idea clearly is plausible.

The class of lags

One of Vygotsky's studies did percolate to the West in the late 1930s and was to influence studies of thinking. In the Vygotsky double block test children are shown 22 wooden blocks. These blocks vary in colour, shape, height and size. On the bottom of each block, one of four words was written in Russian – *lag*, *bik*, *mur* and *sev*. Each of these four nonsense syllables stood for a particular kind of block. Whatever their colour and shape, *lag* was written on all tall, large blocks, *bik* on the flat, large figures, *mur* on the tall, small ones and *sev* on the flat, small ones.

At the start the blocks were scattered all over a board. There were four areas marked on the board. The child had to put all the biks in one area, all the murs in another area and so on.

The experimenter picked up a sample block, showed it to the subject and read its name. After that, participants had to choose all the blocks which belonged to the same class.

Children never sorted the blocks out correctly the first time. At the end of the first go, the experimenter would pick one of the wrongly sorted blocks and read what was on the bottom. Then, they'd encourage the child to do better and start again.

Vygotsky called the method double stimulation and he found an interesting set of patterns in the way children attacked this problem.

Younger children found it hard to form abstract concepts. They had different kinds of preconceptual thinking. First, they grouped blocks together just on the basis of feeling. A child would say a particular number of blocks went together because that's the way it felt to them. Vygotsky called this **syncretic problem solving**. The next major type of grouping, Vygotsky called complex. Here the connections between objects don't just depend on the child's feelings and moods but on some real features of the objects. The child may put all the blue objects together or may suggest that a red shape goes with a blue one. Crucially though the child doesn't extract what is and isn't relevant to the adult way of thinking. That involves distinguishing between essential and non-essential features. For the biks the essential features were large and flat. It was only adolescent children who managed to weed out what the essential features for each group were and so to sort the blocks into the correct biks and lags.

Despite his many differences with Piaget, Vygotsky seemed to have confirmed that only teenagers are capable of formal operations weeding out the essential features of the biks and lags.

The zone of proximal development

Communist societies had tremendous faith in education. The Soviet Union lied about many of its achievements but it did build an extraordinarily successful education system from 1925 on. Vygotsky was interested in whether concept formation in school progresses in the way that his double block test found. Here, there was a real surprise. When children were being asked to learn scientific concepts the Soviets found they were more adept.

In the tradition Piaget came from, the psychologist was a detached observer. Piaget always wanted to know what children thought but he was careful never to help children. He was the scientist, the children were the subjects. He would muddy his experimental results if he helped them.

But Vygotsky thought that children, being naturally social, were at their best in social situations – and often being in social situations where an adult helped them stretched them. He didn't see this as interfering with the natural development of the child but as a natural part of it. Children don't learn in isolation after all.

A study by Roazzi and Bryant (1998) produced an elegant confirmation of Vygotsky's ideas even though the authors never actually mention Vygotsky in their paper. The experimenters gave children aged between about 4 and 5½ years a problem to solve that involved finding out how many sweets were in a box that was put on a set of scales. The young children did the experiments either on their own or with older children present. The older children couldn't tell what the answers were but they could give them clues or suggest they put one box and then another on the scales.

Roazzi and Bryant also did their best to encourage all the children to co-operate. If the young ones got the right answer, they and the others

The Zone of Proximal Development: peers, older siblings, parents or teachers can help children to perform tasks they could not achieve alone. Copyright © Tina Gue/Photofusion.

would all get bags of sweets. They found that social interaction helped the young children crack the problem which they did not manage when they had no help. The zone of proximal development was real enough.

Parents and proximal development

Vygotsky was less concerned with parents but for most children their parents offer an almost constant source of help and encouragement. Mother and father form a zone of proximal development. In the West there's an industry devoted to self-help for parents which assumes sensibly enough that parents are a child's first teachers.

One of my fondest memories is of reading Dr Seuss books like *The CAT in the HAT* to my sons when they were little. Seuss uses clever rhymes, repetition and attractive pictures to drive a story forward. I was having fun with my kids and teaching them at the same time.

Wells (1981) has shown how parents teach children crucial skills involved in talking such as when to take turns to speak. Parents also correct the way children speak, point out new objects and their names to them. It could be argued that this is another example of how young children flourish in social relationships. Mothers and fathers repeat words, speak in a more baby-like way and reward children for understanding and speaking well. The parents are the Zone of Proximal Development, it could be said – and especially in the learning of language.

If you are a parent, you don't have to do anything about this. You certainly don't have to buy a book which gives parents exercises to do with their children. All you need to do is talk to your children, read to them, listen to them.

Vygotsky's stages of development

Vygotsky was far less inclined than Piaget to accept the idea of stages in cognitive development. In a paper published in the Soviet Union in 1962, Vygotksy looked at the notion of 'periodisation' in child development. He argued there were crises in the growth of the child but these crises weren't just a question of the child perfecting their logical abilities. In every crisis, Vygtosky argued, the child gained something and lost something. Piaget saw each stage of development as progress towards adult normality. It was no loss to stop being egocentric. Vygotsky, on the other hand, saw some real losses in the changes. For example, when children were 7 and started to go to full-time school, they often were less able to use a certain whimsical imagination. The more you like facts, the less you love fairy tales, he seemed to assume. (It's one of the many ideas he never actually tested.)

Critiques

Vygotsky hasn't received the almost obsessional detailed critical attention Piaget has. (There are possibly 500 books which offer critiques of Piaget.) As a result it's hard to assess just what the scientific status of his ideas is. He's important as a balance to Piaget. Also the concept of the ZPD makes it clear children can operate with help at a level higher than 'normal' for their stage.

There is a more fundamental critique of stage theories, however. Stage theories assume that at particular points the whole child changes. Is this necessarily true?

Case (1995) has pointed out that one critique of Piaget stemmed from the work of the linguist Noam Chomsky. Chomsky has argued that children's capacity to speak is innate and emerges naturally as long as children are exposed to speech. But language is just one module of the mind.

Some, such as the American psychologists Howard Gardner and Robert Ornstein, have argued one should see all cognitive development in terms of specific domains or modules. Instead of looking for radical shifts in the whole way the child thinks or perceives, one should see the mind as a series of units which may develop at different paces. Unit A, controlling visual perception, may progress tremendously between 2 and 6 months while Unit B, controlling language, doesn't change.

In the 1980s, this view was also held by Case (1985). Case has now modified his thinking on this and we will examine his new ideas at the end of Chapter 5 because he is trying to reconcile Piaget, Vygotsky and just about everything else in the cognitive development field (Case *et al*. 1996). But all these views also need to be re-examined now in terms of the overlapping waves model.

Vygotsky's ideas are an interesting balance to Piaget. Even more than Piaget, however, Vygotsky's studies hardly conform to what are now considered good models of empirical practice. He hardly ever designed studies which attempted to falsify his hypotheses. So is part of his influence due to the very fact that he was neglected for so long?

We have now left the historical greats behind. It's over a century since Piaget and Vygotsky were born and about seventy-five years since they published their key works.

In much of the rest of this book I ask whether their results, massively important as they are, are still wholly valid today given the many social and cultural changes that affect children. In the next chapter, I look at moral development. A key study in understanding that comes from research on how children play marbles. No one has yet used a more modern game like Playstation to see what that might teach us about how children come to understand what is right, what is wrong and what they might be able to get away with.

Siblings teach each other a great deal. The ZPD again! Copyright © Sophie Clausen.

Thinking matter

If you have brothers and/or sisters, think of examples of playing together as children when they taught you or you taught them something.

The development of a moral sense

We have seen in previous chapters how major theories have focused on the intellectual development of children. There is more to growing up than that, however. Since Biblical times, parents and teachers have wanted to teach children how to be good. To say you have a well-brought-up child is still a compliment in Western societies that agonise over issues of morality. At the start of the twenty-first century, however, countries like Britain and America are having to grapple with the fact that children whom we tend to idealise as innocent are often involved not just in bad behaviour – breaking windows when playing football – but in serious crimes. The question of when children know right from wrong is no longer just an academic one but one that courts and lawyers have to decide.

In this chapter I look at:

- **theories of moral development such as those of Piaget and Kohlberg**

- **the question of whether these now rather ancient theories fit contemporary experiences**

- **how children learn about rules**

- **how children perceive what is right and what is wrong**

- **what punishments seem just for what offence**

- **the relationship between how children learn about rules and justice and their cognitive development**.

Traditionally English law claimed that children under the age of 10 were incapable of knowing the difference between right and wrong. Copyright © Gina Glover/Photofusion.

Psychologists have been concerned with delinquent children since the late nineteenth century. A psychoanalyst August Aichhorn (1878–1949) set up two training centres in Austria for reforming them. Britain introduced borstals – institutes for young deliquents – early in the twentieth century – and a splendid description of life in them in the 1920s was given by an inmate Mark Benney in his book *Low Company*. Bullying and pressure to have sex with older boys were routine then but nearly all the delinquents psychologists dealt with were in their mid-teens or older.

Younger criminals

Today, children commit crimes at a younger age. A number of high-profile cases like the murder of James Bulger by two boys who were aged 10 and 11 have made the issue topical. It is no longer exceptional for children under the age of 11 to be tried for serious crimes. The number of crimes in Britain committed by children aged 10 and 11 is around 1000 per 100 000 of the population for boys and 230 per 100 000 for girls (1999 figures produced by the Home Office). The preteen criminal is common now. Palermo and Ross (1999) looked at cases of mass murder in the states and found that between 1994 and 1996 there had been six cases of juveniles gunning down a number of people. It is widely believed, however, that the British statistics underestimate reality. Many child criminals are not caught; sometimes, those who are caught never come into contact with the criminal justice system. They are dealt with by social services. In a film I made for Channel 4's *Dispatches* in 1991, I reported that one third of all cases of sexual abuse are committed by children and young people under the age of 18. I collected a number of interviews with abusers who said that they themselves had been abused very young and had often started abusing children when they were under the age of 10. Few of these young abusers had ever been tried.

Traditionally English law claimed that children under the age of 10 were incapable of knowing the difference between right and wrong.To be found guilty of a crime, a person had to have the intention or *mens rea* to commit it. A person who was too young to form such an intention to do wrong could not be guilty of a criminal offence. That person might still need to be detained in, for example, a special hospital like Broadmoor for the safety of the public but they could not be found guilty of a crime. Children, idiots and the insane couldn't judge either the consequences of their actions or what was right or wrong.

Today, we are much more ambivalent. We want to cling to the idea that children are innocent but we are constantly being confronted by dramas which suggest otherwise.

The defence in the Bulger case, for example, did not argue his killers were so young that they didn't know that killing a child was wrong. Many television documentaries, in particular, have followed young children on the streets and reported on the offences they commit. The tabloids at the end of 1999 carried a story about a 5-year-old drug dealer and asked whether that child was the youngest drug dealer in the country.

Psychologists have, I shall argue, grappled rather ineffectively with the question of the moral development of children. The two main theorists – Piaget, again, and the American Lawrence Kohlberg – seem to have studied the issue in a way that now seems to us almost naive. Part of the naiveté stems from the fact that Piaget's Switzerland in the 1920s either was a very different society or was perceived as such. I am tempted to think the latter is true and that much was kept secret. The therapist Carl Rogers worked for the Society for the Prevention of Cruelty to Children in upstate New York, from 1929 to 1940. Rogers left his papers to the Library of Congress in Washington DC and among his notes are case histories of children who would be utterly familiar to social services departments today. One of the first children to make an impression on Rogers was a 7-year-old boy called John. John presented as a very sexually aggressive child. He had molested two little girls and introduced a number of boys to 'sex perversion', Rogers noted. One of the first questions John asked Rogers was whether the therapist slept with his wife.

Such extreme cases do not figure in the psychological literature on moral development, as Piaget and other leading theorists wrote it. Rogers himself downplayed what we would see as cases of child abuse (Cohen 1997). We are faced again with the possibility that the leading theories on offer are not so much wrong as just out of date. The most modern example I can find in Piaget's work involves children being told a story about a younger boy and an older boy who bullies him at school. Piaget asked a number of 6- to 8-year-olds what they thought when the younger boy responded by stealing the sandwich and apple the older bully brought to school. In the world of Lara Croft and Donkey Kong the stolen apple doesn't usually feature much. Bullying remains a very real problem in schools but many children now have to face even greater ones like drugs.

In the Introduction I argued that exposure to the media and social changes including changes in family structure may be having a variety of effects on children's development. Take three basic facts. It has been estimated that the average child watches over twenty hours of television a week. Much of that viewing will be contemporary soaps and dramas which involve battles that pit goodies against baddies. The viewer is constantly looking at situations where it is very clear what is right and what is wrong. Second, one marriage in two in Britain ends in divorce. It has been estimated that perhaps 2 million British children grow up in stepfamilies. They will have heard bitter arguments between parents; they will be living in complex extended families where they will see parents take the sides of their own children, for example, against others in the family. Third, it has been estimated that 20 per cent of children under the age of 14 will have experimented with drugs. Such factors are bound to affect the moral development of children.

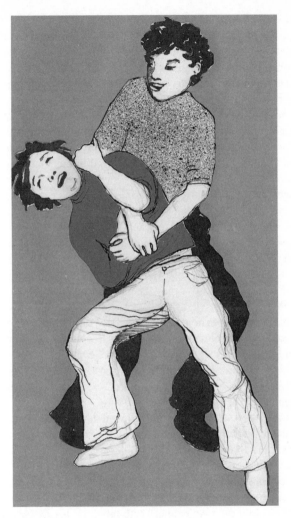

Bullying or tickling? Copyright © Sophie Clausen

A case of losing your marbles? Piaget and moral development

Piaget attacked the topic of moral development as an extension of his work on cognitive development. His key writings on the subjects are his book *The Moral Judgement of the Child*, first published in 1929 and translated into English in 1932, and certain sections of *Play, Dreams and Imitation in Children*. Piaget deals with a range of subjects: the rules of marbles, children's sense of justice, what they regard as reasonable punishments for particular offences. If you tease your younger brother mercilessly is your father right to smack you? As ever Piaget tries to impose order and unity on a wide spread of material. Piaget noted that for the children a pure Calvinist morality ruled. The Ten Commandments were taught in the family and in Church. 'Thou shalt not' ruled. Authority had to be obeyed in this black and white world.

Piaget started his inquiry in a charming way. Ten years after he had wandered round Neufchatel looking at the pond life, he wandered around playgrounds. He set out to observe how children played marbles; he studied local variations of the game between Geneva and Neufchatel. Once he had noted the basic rules of marbles in real life, Piaget began his experiments. He gave marbles to children and told them he had no idea how to play the game. Would they show him the rules? He noted the answers they gave him and then, true to his clinical method, he asked questions. This procedure meant that Piaget had to make a doubtful assumption – that when he told the children he did not know the rules of marbles, they believed him. Yet marbles was an ancient game, handed down from generation to generation. Why should Piaget, an adult born in the area, not know the rules? The question never seems to have bothered him.

His interviews with children allowed him to put forward the following hypothesis. The moral judgement of the child passes through stages similar to those of intellectual development. At first the child throws marbles, makes them push each other and toys with them. It may look like playing marbles but the child is, according to Piaget, just following 'motor rules', his or her individual rituals of the game. The child does not connect with others; is hardly playing with others.

At the age of 3, the child reaches a higher level of play. He begins to follow the rules that he has seen his elders practise. For example, if a 3-year-old sees that each player has three marbles, the 3- or 4-year-old will assert that the proper way to play is with three marbles. The best that the 3 to 4-year-old can do, Piaget suggests, is to play according to a very individual notion of the rules. Piaget compares moral development with intellectual development. And Eureka! Egocentricity rules in the playground as well.

Proper collaboration between children, the kind that is needed to play a game with others, doesn't start to be found before 4 to 6 years of age. Even then the child is usually playing to his own variable rules. Piaget again makes the comparison between intellectual and moral development. He stresses that though the child seems to be playing with other children, he cannot in reality pay sufficient attention to them, to the rules, or to others points of view to really play with them.

Piaget detected a change round the age of 7. By then the child knows the rules of the game well enough to follow them and to play a legal game of marbles. Piaget compares this – and it is for him a vital comparison – to the transition in cognitive development from the pre-operational stage to that of concrete operations. The concrete child is no longer so egocentric. He may not be able to grasp the theory behind conservation but he knows that if the same liquid is poured from a big fat pot to a tall thin pot it is the same amount of liquid. Piaget claims concrete children also have a very fixed notion of rules in the game of marbles. In writing about Piaget, Flavell (1962) wrote that the child saw the rules as almost sacred without being able to explain them properly. Ten-year-olds typically move on from this paradoxical position.

The next stage occurs around 11 when the child becomes able not just to play according to the rules but also to explain them. He becomes a person who follows rules he can understand and, if necessary, justify. The child becomes a moral being who can judge whether rules are right or wrong or sensible. Intellect precedes ethics, Piaget argued in effect.

Children's conceptions of justice

Piaget found interesting patterns, too, in children's attitudes to lies and to justice. Young children, aged 3 or 4, were not interested in the consequences of actions but in simple quantity. It was worse to break fifteen cups than to break just one. Motivation did not matter; nor did intention; nor did mitigating circumstances. Yet one of the key factors in judging people's actions is our intention. If I kill my wife by accident, making her a prawn curry which just happens to contain toxic prawns, a court will find me innocent of murder. If, on the other hand, I sprinkle arsenic on the prawns I will be guilty, even if she recovers. For young children, Piaget found, there are no such distinctions. The idea that intentions are crucial only starts to appear at the age of about 7 to 8.

Piaget also found children's attitudes to lies interesting. At 3 or 4 children see lying, as saying something which is forbidden like a swear word. Around the age of 5, the lie is seen simply as something that is not true. Piaget also argued that the further away the truth, the greater the lie as children see it. It was more of a lie to say I was arriving on Monday and turn up on Wednesday than if I turned up on Tuesday. If I arrived on Wednesday, the lie would be 24 hours bigger. Again a matter of quantity; mitigating circumstances did not matter. If I did my best to get there on Monday but my train was cancelled because there were the wrong kind of leaves on the line, the classic railway excuse, it did not alter the way a 5-year-old would see it. Never mind, I still lied. I was not there on Monday.

Towards the age of 9 children change. They come to see that intentions are a crucial factor in the equation. If I lie to be nice or to be moral then I have some excuses for my lies.

In exploring the idea of justice, Piaget offered an account of how children's sense of justice evolved. He gave children a story about a big boy who bullies a little boy in school and sometimes beats him. The small one does not have the guts to fight the bigger boy – notice in this scenario no one draws a knife, let alone a gun as can be the case now in American schools – so instead, to get some revenge, the victim hides the sandwich and apple the bully brings to school for lunch. Piaget captured the following reactions.

Mon (6½ years) 'He ought to do it.' *Why?*, 'Because the big one always hit him.'

A 7-year-old Aud, agreed saying that the little boy did well and that his brother should not have been hitting him. Aud, Piaget noted, did not understand the word 'revenge' but added that it was not a bad thing to do. Another 7-year-old Hel said it was 'all right to do it . . . because the big one messed him up'.

By the age of 10, children were more complex in their justifications. It was not just that the little boy was right to do it but that there was an underlying principle that 'big boys mustn't hit little boys,' as Ag put it.

Piaget offered two slightly different interpretations of his findings. The weak case was that moral and intellectual development evolved in parallel. The strong case that he often made was that intellectual development determined moral development. The moral realism, as he put it, of the young child who thinks breaking fifteen cups is worse, whatever the circumstances, than breaking one cup is due to ego-centricity, to being bound by immediate perceptions. Before the age of 8, before they get into concrete operations, children see rules as fixed, divine, unchangeable. Piaget argued that children evolved from such rigid attitudes. After the age of 8, children began to integrate into a final judgement of situations all the calculations adults make when they come to ethical decisions – the intentions, motives, reasons and excuses that drive actions.

Piaget offers an excellent model of how adults can talk about complex themes with children even if he lived in a much more innocent culture. Some research by Dunn and Cutting (1999) has found that children as young as 4 make interesting distinctions about issues such as whether it is all right for someone who is a friend to borrow a toy of yours without asking. I wouldn't presume to give parents or professionals a list of topics to discuss with their kids but the daily news provides endless starters for moral conversations – both at home and in class.

There has been far less critical discussion of Piaget's moral development than of his cognitive theories but his work was built on by Lawrence Kohlberg who spent thirty years developing a linked theory.

Kohlberg's dilemmas

Kohlberg started on the subject with his doctoral thesis in 1955. This turned into a longitudinal study of 50 American males who were aged between 10 and 26 at the start of the research. The subjects were re-interviewed every three years. Kohlberg asked them questions such as why you should not steal from a store; he also presented them with a series of dilemmas.

One of the best known of these dilemmas is that of Heinz and the druggist. Heinz's wife was near death as a result of a cancer. Her doctor thought one drug might save her. A biochemist had just discovered a new form of radium. The drug was expensive to make. It cost him $200 for a course of treatment but the biochemist charged $2,000. The sick woman's husband, Heinz, went to everyone he knew to borrow money but the most he could raise was $1,000. He asked the biochemist either to sell him the drug more cheaply or to let him pay later. The stubborn biochemist refused. He had invented the drug and he wanted to make money from it. So the desperate Heinz broke into the lab and stole some of the drug.

Kohlberg asked his subjects whether Heinz was justified in robbing the biochemist. If so, why? If not, why not?

On the basis of these answers, Kohlberg argued there were three levels of moral reasoning – and each level had two stages. The first stage is that of pre-conventional morality. Typically a subject would say that one should not steal from a store because it was against the law – and the police might catch you. The second stage was more individual. It was acceptable to steal either to meet one's immediate needs or interests or because of reciprocal relationships. For example, if someone behaved badly to you, you would be justified in behaving badly to them.

The second level was that of conventional morality. You lived up to what people expected of you in your role. Being good mattered and included having good motives. In the second stage of conventional morality, subjects are aware of laws and of the fact that laws need to be upheld for society to function.

The third level of post-conventional thinking, Kohlberg argues, is reached by only a minority of adults – and nearly always after the age of 20. They accept that laws have to be upheld but there are exceptional circumstances, reasons of principle where it is acceptable to break the law for moral reasons. Kohlberg speaks of universal ethical principles. Many of the post-conventional thinkers would agree that Heinz was justified in stealing the rare drug, and not just because it was a matter of life and death but also because the biochemist was so greedy and uncaring. He had it coming.

Like Piaget, Kohlberg accepts that the level of moral reasoning a child reaches depends on his, or her, cognitive development. He suggested that someone at the level of concrete operations would be at the pre-conventional stage of moral reasoning, that a child just starting to master formal operations would be in the conventional stage of moral reasoning and that the formal child would be in the post-conventional stage.

Are mathematicians more moral?

There is an interesting anomaly here. Bradmetz (1999) found that only one out of sixty-two 15-year-olds seem ever to really master formal operations and Precheur (1976) found that only 4 per cent of 18-year-olds doing literary studies mastered formal operations. If moral reasoning were dependent on cognitive development and only mathematically trained youngsters ever reached formal operations, then it should follow that the vast majority of those who make moral decisions based on universal principles should turn out to be mathematicians. The subject hasn't been formally studied to my knowledge and one has to rely on anecdotes. One of the great conscientious objectors of the twentieth century was Bertrand Russell, co-author of the *Principia Mathematica* and, we presume, someone who had reached the stage of formal operations. But Russell behaved badly to his wives and children according to a recent biography (Monk 1999). Einstein also famously had second thoughts about developing the atom bomb and pleaded for it not to be used. A new biography suggests, however, Einstein had – and caused – endless troubles with women. Mathematicians are like everyone else, but better at figures.

There is no evidence that the majority of conscientious objectors in the First World War and Second World War were mathematicians and logicians who would be able to argue convincingly that a universal ethic justified them in not killing others. Much anecdotal evidence goes the other way. For example, some of the most famous cries of conscience in the First World War came from poets like Siegfried Sassoon. In papers just released by the Public Record Office for 1949, we learn that the playwright Harold Pinter fought two court cases that year, not to be called up, on conscientious grounds. The development of weapons of mass destruction in the twentieth century depended, in fact, on physicists and mathematicians; the great majority went along with it, cocooned their consciences even though they were well aware of the destruction it would cause. The link between mathematical skill, mastery of formal operations and a profound moral sense is one which needs to be proved. The absence of such evidence makes one doubt whether a highly developed moral sense actually requires the logical competence Piaget and Kohlberg claimed. It's an issue researchers ought to address.

There have been many other criticisms of Kohlberg's research. First, he has little to say about children who are under 10. In the 1950s that might have been acceptable but the huge increase in pre-teen crime in Britain and the United States suggests we need to know much more about knowledge of right and wrong in younger children. Kurtines and Greif (1974), for example, pointed out that the dilemmas were very subjective and scores between them did not intercorrelate particularly well. So, a child might be very conventional about Heinz's dilemma and very post-conventional about a different scenario.

Damon(1977) asked just how realistic dilemmas such as Heinz's might seem to a 10-year-old or a 17-year-old. He listened to the arguments of children and made up a number of dilemmas of his own. In one a class paints pictures. The teacher thinks they are so good he suggests the class sell them at a fair. How should the class divide the money? Should it be equally divided or should a child who sells his picture get to keep the money paid for it even though he only did it as part of a class effort? Damon found that there were key differences between the 10- and 17-year-olds. The 10-year-olds tended to be less selfish and believe the class should share equally.

There are also some intriguing studies that suggest today's children are better able to see some of the moral issues involved in lying from an early age.

Lies and leakage

Turliel (1983) argued that Kohlberg had provided interesting information on how children see rules but found that children as young as 4 had a natural sense of justice. He suggested there was evidence that these children might not always be able to follow rules but that they did often have a notion of what was right or wrong.

In some amusing work on lying – his subject was mainly his own daughter – Stephen Ceci, professor at Cornell and a leading child psychologist, suggests that children as young as 5 are uncomfortable about lying because they know it is wrong. At a seminar in London in 1998, he gave two interesting pieces of evidence for that. First he took his daughter to visit her mother in hospital. The hospital rules forbade children younger than 6 visiting. Ceci told his daughter that if anyone asked her age she should say it was 6. When a friendly nurse asked the daughter how old she was, she replied, 'He said I should say I was six.' Ceci suggested that perhaps psychologists are not so good at teaching children about deception.

Ceci also filmed his daughter after deliberately placing her in a tricky moral situation. She had seen him steal some toy trucks and he had told her not to tell on him. Ceci then left her alone and a friend of theirs appeared. She had been briefed by Ceci, of course, and started to question his daughter. Told by Daddy not to expose him as a toy thief, when she was asked what had happened, lied. Ceci's daughter said her father had not touched the trucks but her body language showed, Ceci argued, all the classic signs of nervousness and anxiety. 'She showed lots of leakage,' Ceci said. His daughter was uncomfortable about lying because she knew it was wrong but her father had asked her to protect him – and so she lied.

The dynamic that Ceci explored in these charming anecdotes is also a dynamic that fuels much darker scenarios. Social workers dealing with child abuse know that children will often keep quiet or lie about what adults do to them – and they lie for very adult reasons. The children know that what has been happening is wrong, they often hate being abused but they do not want to get their father in trouble or cause their mother pain. Ceci offered the 1998 seminar many poignant examples of such cases.

I am not suggesting that there was no sexual abuse before 1970 but it was certainly not an issue psychologists highlighted. Carl Rogers, the humanist therapist, listed the various problems children in Rochester, New York suffered from at the start of 1930. Of those in his care 20 suffered from 'adolescent restlessness', 28 suffered from 'poor habit training', 28 had 'poor companions' but Rogers noted only one case where he suspected parents might have corrupted a child's moral sense. Rogers was writing at the time Piaget was developing his theory of moral reasoning. This failure to relate theory to what was happening to children in less salubrious settings than the marble-playing fields of Switzerland has made Piaget's theories seem a little too fairy-tale like.

Intention and intention to deceive

The notion of intention is central to this. Harré has argued that children are capable of framing intentions far younger than we had realised. Harré was my external examiner for my Ph.D. thesis. In that thesis

I argued that some of my subjects had, by the age of 24 months, the intention to do something funny, an observation that Harré suggested to me was important. Being able to intend an action is, of course, very different from seeing intentions in the behaviour of others.

A much more recent and systematic study by Joseph and Tager Flusberg(1999) has summarised how much children understand of intentions. They gave children a set of stories in which characters behaved in a number of unexceptional ways. The characters climbed fences, for example, to get into a field. The psychologists then asked the children questions which were meant to explore whether or not the children understood the concept of intention. They differentiated between intention based on knowledge and intention based on desire as when a child says 'I want a sweet' and then takes one from the kitchen cupboard. They found that over 70 per cent of 3-year-olds were quite capable of understanding the link between wanting, intention and action. They concluded that children grasp the idea of agency and intention younger than has been realised. Their findings suggest that when children do something wrong they have a reasonable sense of the significance of what they are doing.

In sum, the traditional theories of moral development seem very much out of fit both with the realities of life in present-day society and with what we know about how children perceive and understand intention. We have a paradoxical situation. On the one hand, children commit more crimes and they do so younger. On the other hand, they seem to have a better developed sense of what is right and what is wrong than psychologists have allowed.

In the next chapter I look at the research on social and emotional development which suggests that children develop an understanding of other minds earlier than was previously thought – and much of that research hinges on how children can pretend and deceive.

5

Other people and other minds

A baby's crying. His parents wake up. They're tired but they pick him up and comfort him. Does this prove babies have social intelligence and 'know' crying will make their parents hug them? Or is it just that the human newborn is innately 'wired' to cry? It's just a reflex. Two-year-olds certainly know if they cry, good parents will give them attention.

Piaget often ignored the social intelligence of babies and young children. Yet to observers it is often one of their most obvious and endearing characteristics. In this chapter we're going to examine:

- **how children start to describe mental states, i.e. when they first start to say 'I want' or 'I think'**

- **how children start to realise other people have minds of their own**

- **children's understanding of pretending**

- **how children seem to develop an understanding of psychology itself**

- **Robbie Case's ambitious attempt to marry Piaget, Vygotsky and recent work on the theory of mind.**

One of the most exciting recent developments in cognitive development has been work on how children come to understand thinking, emotion and the brain itself. We saw earlier Chomsky argue the human brain may never be able to understand how the human brain works. Yet curiously the work of Paul Harris and Henry Wellman and their colleagues has made it clear that children start to develop the ability to think about other people as other people certainly by the age of 3. Some findings suggest even 18-month-olds can grasp some elements of other minds. Such research forces us to reconsider Piaget's key notion of egocentricity; children who can ascribe motives to others can hardly be said to be egocentric.

Henry Wellman of the University of Michigan, who has studied the field for some twenty years, attributes children's increased psychological sophistication to 'a much wider range of exposure to social interaction. Children go to day care, they don't live in nuclear families, they engage much more in pretend play and that has an effect.' In an interview for the *New Scientist*, he insisted that children communicate far more with other people at younger ages than they did in the past. It grows them up.

Does increased exposure to social interaction at younger ages make children more psychologically sophisticated? Copyright © Andrew Parker/ Photofusion.

With older children the facts are even more perplexing. Many teenagers and adults never master formal operations, but children seem to become more emotionally aware younger. Magazines for the pre-teen market such as *Jackie* assume children as young as 12 'date' and understand complex aspects of adult relationships.

Let's start with a typical teenage scene. Bridget and Doug are 13 and are dating. As they're out seeing a movie, Doug goes all moody and silent.

'I thought you were happy,' Bridget complains.
'You don't have a clue what I feel,' Doug complains back.
'How can I, if you don't talk . . .'

Doug pauses. He's going to make the most of this moment. 'I'm worried about my Dad. He's depressed,' Doug finally says.

Understanding knots in human relationships

Back in the hippie 1960s, the radical psychiatrist R.D. Laing wrote *Knots* which examined the tangle of human relationships in brief poems and scenarios.

JILL: I'm upset that you are upset.
JACK: I'm not upset.
JILL: I'm upset that you're not upset because I'm upset you're upset.
JACK: I'm upset that you're upset that I'm not upset that you're upset that I'm upset when I'm not.

Laing called his characters Jack and Jill to highlight how childish these adult games were.

Social beings

From the moment we're born we live among others. Every hour we respond to other people. We try to work out how other people are feeling and very often what they're thinking and what they're thinking of us. This isn't a question of those much over-used words **insight** or **intuition**. We just can't live without other people. 'Only connect,' wrote the novelist E.M. Forster as a guide to happiness.

Sometimes, psychology responds slowly to shifts in popular culture. Once upon a time the British were famous for not talking about their feelings. It was an uptight land of bowlers, brollies and cream teas. The classic Brit-feel film was Noel Coward's *Brief Encounter*. Two married people meet, fall in love and nothing happens. (Much of the action or inaction takes place in a railway station buffet.) Today Brits are more willing to talk about feelings – and this should affect children.

Only in the last ten years have psychologists started to talk about **interpersonal intelligence**, intelligence about other people or emotional intelligence, as Daniel Goleman called his international bestseller (1992). Even these concepts don't quite catch the complexities of how people live and think about relationships in postmodern, post-Freudian societies.

In *The Romantic Movement* (1998) Alain de Botton has written an acute novel on contemporary intricacies of relationships. De Botton's heroine falls in love with a man who doesn't merely lack insight but who is emotionally blind, deaf and dumb. He never has the slightest idea what his lover feels or thinks so he's astonished when she leaves him because of his lack of emotional intelligence. The lover is logically mature and psychologically about 6 years old, a combination never contemplated by Piaget.

Many psychologists realised in the 1980s that the traditional concept of intelligence was too narrow. In his list of multiple intelligences, Howard Gardner includes:

Interpersonal intelligence – how we think about other people.

Intrapersonal intelligence – how we think about ourselves.

Robert Sternberg also argued we need to include social intelligence among the intelligences.

How do children develop these cognitive skills? To understand the debate it's necessary to understand what we mean by **mental states**. A mental state is a state of mind. Some of the most common mental states psychologists discuss are believing, hoping, liking, desiring.

Children's use of verbs that reflect mental states

There's no foolproof way of knowing when children start to realise they have mental states because by definition a mental state can't be observed. It is inside your mind. Psychologists have concentrated instead on observable behaviours such as when infants begin to use verbs that reflect mental states. (These studies deal with the development of both language and psychological sense but most psychologists concentrate on what they reveal about the latter.) When a child says 'I want', 'I think', 'I believe', 'I wish', 'I dream', 'I like' and so on, we assume that child is expressing the fact they're experiencing the relevant mental state of wanting, believing or dreaming (Huttenlocher, Smiley and Chaney, 1983).

No 6-month-old baby can say the words 'I want'; most 2-year-old toddlers say it regularly.

We still don't really know how infants start to use phrases such as 'I wish' but we can plot better than ever before the changes that happen after 2 years of age, changes that make most 4- and 5-year-olds surprisingly competent social operators.

Exercise in self-observation

Again do some introspection.

What is your first memory of doing something because you thought it would please your parents?

What is your first memory of doing something because you thought you could get away with it?

There's no reason to suppose your memories will be accurate but the age you think you first used such words is still interesting. Virtually no one will assume their first such memories will come from as late as 10.

How children understand emotions

I remember the following set of events when I was between 6 and 7. I lived in Geneva. I was in a park playing with a gun. Another boy came up to me and asked if he could play with my gun. When I wouldn't give it, the boy got his father. His father told me it was selfish not to share. Then, he asked my name.

'David Cohen,' I said.
'Filthy Jew,' he said.

I ran home, crying. My father asked what was wrong. I explained. My father put his coat on and announced he'd give the anti-Semite a 'good hiding'. My mother was scared. She said that as Jews and foreigners, we were in no position to make scenes. The man was obviously Swiss and he might call the police. I remember vividly being torn between my parents and understanding both their feelings – his anger and her fear.

I don't believe my reactions were unusual. Research on children in families who divorce shows they often understand the tensions in the family. They resent the fact their parents assume they're too young to understand and so don't talk to them about what is going on. Dasgupta (1998) has argued parents must not underestimate the emotional awareness of children aged 6 and upwards.

Imitation and awareness

The first sign of awareness of other people comes from evidence that babies can imitate the actions of others. When we think what imitation means, it's reasonable to argue that to imitate you, first, I have to notice you are there; second, I have to perceive your actions; third, I have to have the conscious ability to reproduce or parody them. Some psychologists place studies of imitation in the context of the development of memory. It is to some extent a matter of taste. Since many of the actions imitated are social, I deal with the topic here.

In *Play, Dreams and Imitation*, Piaget (1952) suggested the first imitations were vocal. One child, T, at 2 months 11 days uttered the sounds 'la' and 'le'. 'I reproduced them. He repeated them seven times out of nine slowly and distinctly' (p. 9). Piaget was not sure whether these imitations were pure reflexes or meant more. By the age of 4 to 5 months, he was sure such imitations were signs of some intelligence. At 5 months one of his daughters, J, was certainly imitating him. When he put out his tongue at her, she then put out her tongue at him.

The British psychologist C.W. Valentine also suggested first imitations were vocal. He would whimper at his nearly 2-month-old son and the baby would whimper back.

The real shock came in the 1980s when research suggested babies were able to imitate adults literally 30 minutes after they were born. Meltzoff and Moore (1983) found newborn babies could imitate an adult opening their mouth and sticking out their tongue sometimes when they were just 30 minutes old. They found this 'skill' lasted sometimes till 21 days – and that usually babies imitated movements.

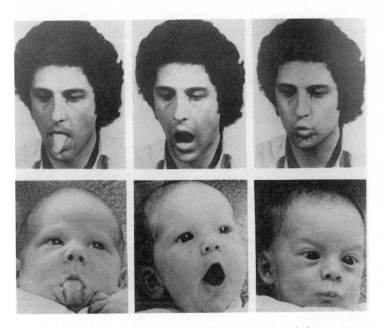

Meltzoff and Moore (1977) showed that newborns can imitate tongue protrusion, mouth opening and lip pursing movements. Reprinted with permission from A.N. Meltzoff and M.K. Moore (1977), Imitation of facial and manual gestures by human neonates. *Science, 198*, 75–78. Copyright © 1977 American Association for the Advancement of Science. Courtesy of A.N. Meltzoff.

Reissland in a study of Nepalese babies (1988) found they too could imitate an adult sticking out the tongue or pursing his lips or widening his lips. At about 3 weeks of age, babies temporarily lost this skill but it reappeared a few months later.

The question is what do these imitations mean? Could they be a kind of reflex? If so, it's a very different reflex because it's not triggered by a sound like head turning, or by a sensation like grasping an object put in the hand. Rather the imitation is triggered by a stimulus which is, in some sense, social.

Imitation becomes more complex after 9 months. Piaget saw children under 12 months imitating adults waving goodbye. Possibly the most interesting tester of imitation was C.W. Valentine. When one of his children was 13 months old, Valentine started an intensive series of tests of imitation. It included things like tearing a newspaper and putting a basket over his head. In 31 cases out of 37 he found his 1-year-old imitated the actions.

When a 6-year-old imitates Batman, he can explain what he's doing and why. Babies are unlikely to be thinking 'Ah here's this weird adult doing this weird thing. I'm going to imitate him.' Babies half an hour after they're born can't – or we assume they can't – have intentions or ideas.

These observations, however, suggest newborn babies have some kind of mental representation which allows them to perceive an adult is poking the tongue out, to identify the tongue as the focus of that behaviour and to activate the muscles of their own tongue so that it pokes out too. In general, psychologists tend to report this behaviour rather than to explain what it means. If you follow the logic, the conclusion is too incredible – attributing a degree of impossible sophistication to babies.

Nevertheless, the evidence suggests babies, and even newborns, do respond to other people. This leads to a complex issue: the child's theory of mind. Piaget wanted us to see the child as an apprentice logician; there is growing evidence the child is also an apprentice psychologist – and much better at that than at logic.

A mind of her own

Some of the most persuasive evidence has been put together by Karen Bartsch and Henry Wellman, American psychologists who have analysed some 200,000 utterances between children and their parents. The sample of children they studied was small – only ten children. But the study was longitudinal and followed children from 18 months to 6 years.

In '*Children Talk About the Mind*', Bartsch and Wellman (1995) argue that an excellent way of understanding what children think about feelings, wishes and thoughts is to listen to their conversations. Their book often seems like eavesdropping.

By the age of 4, all their ten children were capable of the following kinds of exchange:

ROSS (3 years 10 months):   Leslie makes me angry.
ADULT: Why?

ROSS: If she thinks something is silly. I don't think it's silly at all.
ADULT: Oh, you had a disagreement?
ROSS: Uh huh, she thought her necklace was silly.
ADULT: She thought it was silly?
ROSS: Yeah. But I didn't think it was.

Ross clearly understands Leslie has a mind of her own and that her mental state differs from his own. When he is questioned by the adult, Ross explains the situation well. He and Leslie disagree about the necklace. When the adult puts to Ross what he understands Ross to have thought about Leslie's view of the necklace, Ross again responds quite appropriately. He spells out again he and Leslie have different thoughts and feelings about the necklace.

Most of the 200,000 child utterances were conversations between parents and children. Young children, the authors claim, are most at ease when talking with their parents and so are likely to develop those conversations more. One child's conversations were recorded from when he was just 10 months old, one girl from when she was 16 months old. All the other children were between 18 months and 2 years 6 months when the recordings started. Bartsch and Wellman couldn't be sure that they had caught the earliest examples of language about mental states.

Bartsch and Wellman looked separately at **references to thoughts and beliefs** and at **references to feelings and desires**.

I wish, I want, I like

A little to their surprise, Bartsch and Wellman found evidence of talk of desires from 18 months. The first children to use desire terms were Eve and Mark, both of whom were 18 months old. In Eve's case they argued this was a genuine reference; in Mark's case they were less sure.

In their report, they offer instances of what they believe constitutes appropriate talk of desires. Unfortunately, they do not actually quote Eve's 18-months-old conversation.

This is one of the conversations they do report. When he was 2 years 5 months, Abe heard his mother ask his father if he enjoyed the cranberry muffin. Abe then added 'I wanna cranberry muffin. I like them.'

Abe was not just expressing a want but offering some psychological explanation for his desire. He wants a cranberry muffin because he likes them.

A slightly more elaborate conversation took place when a little boy called Ross who was 2 years 6 months was scratched by another boy.

ROSS: I want a Band Aid. The boy hurt me.
ADULT: The boy hurt you? How did the boy hurt you?
ROSS: The boy wanted to.

Ross doesn't answer the question he's being asked but he has no doubt that the boy intended to hurt him. It's impossible not to admit that Ross has the capacity to attribute a mental state to his aggressor.

Valentine (1942) had noted something similar in one of his children, B. He suddenly put his arms round his mother and said 'B likes Mummie' and kissed her spontaneously. Valentine thought his child had previously only heard 'like' being used in reference to things that were to be eaten. The next day B came up to Valentine in the garden, put his arms around his neck and said 'B likes Daddie'.

Bartsch and Wellman suggest that by the age of 3 years, children seem well able to talk about wishes and desires in a 'correct' way. This fits in with the work on intention covered in the previous chapter. Their analyses suggest a progression. Children master the basic vocabulary first; more subtle expressions enter children's conversation in the next year. A 3-year-old is unlikely to use expressions such as 'I hope' while a 4-year-old is quite likely to.

I think, therefore I am – again

One of the most interesting – but not surprising – findings is that young children start to refer to thoughts and beliefs later than they refer to desires and emotions. Valentine recorded very few instances of his children talking about thoughts. Bartsch and Wellman calculated that about one in every 120 utterances by a child concerned thoughts or beliefs. Utterances about desires and wishes were far more frequent – about one in every 40.

Nevertheless Bartsch and Wellman (1995) found some instances of such talk just before children reached the age of 3. They suggest there are three different uses of 'I think'.

- 'I think he's a nasty piece of work' where thought is a belief. You could just as easily say 'I believe he's a nasty piece of work';

- 'I thought my hands are paper' where thinking is a form of imagination;
- Thinking as an activity.

One of the earliest conversations to mention thinking that Bartsch and Wellman report features thinking in this sense of an activity.

ADAM (2 years 11 months): I . . . just thinking.
ADULT: You're just thinking?
ADAM: Yes.
ADULT: What are you thinking about?
ADAM: Thinking 'bout leaf.

Slowly children started to use words such as 'wonder', 'expect', 'hope', etc.

There were over 4,500 uses of these verbs. Of these 40 per cent were genuine psychological utterances.

For every child, belief references were found by the age of 3.5 years. The average was at 2 years 9 months.

Just how much does the research suggest 4-year-olds know?

Wellman also looked at references to other mental states. The researchers found children always had more utterances about their own mental states than about the mental states of other people. Only 21 per cent of the references were to someone else's mental states.

The surprise was that some of these references did appear when the children were extremely young. In the case of Adam, Wellman and his colleagues found the first references to others' thoughts at the age of 3 years. In the case of Abe it was at the age of 2 years and 10 months.

False beliefs

The philosopher Gilbert Ryle argued that philosophers should not get too interested in pretending because when we pretend we know that what we are doing is not real and that it is an activity that can only occur when we already have a good sense of reality. But child psychologists have in the last twenty years become very interested in how children pretend; especially as children who do not play pretend games seem to be at risk of autism (Happé 1995), psychologists have also developed a form of experiment which illuminates what children think or believe about what other people think or believe.

These experiments are called false belief studies. The typical situation is simple. A child is shown two dolls – John and Sally. John hides an object behind a sofa. Sally is then taken out of the room. While Sally is out of the room, the object is taken from behind the sofa and hidden in a box. John, who has either seen this happen or done it, knows where the object now is. But Sally does not. Logically when she comes back, she believes the object is still behind the sofa.

Before the age of 3, if a child is asked where Sally will look for the object, typically the child will say that she will search in the box. The child does not understand that since the object was moved when Sally was not there, Sally has no reason to search in the box. Between 3 and 4 years of age, however, children change. They get the idea that Sally thinks the object is where she last saw it. The fact that they know where the object really is is irrelevant. They can see into Sally's mind, if you like, and they know that Sally will have a false belief for perfectly good reasons. So she will look for the object where she saw it hidden.

Recent studies have shown that the instructions one gives children matter. If they are asked where Sally will look first, 71 per cent of 3-year-olds in one study got the answer right (Joseph and Tager Flusberg 1999). In the same study 94 per cent of 4-year-olds got it right.

Another form of situation is when 3-, 4- and 5-year-olds are shown a distinctive candy box that actually contains pencils. The subjects are then shown the box has no sweets. Perner (1999) found that children from the age of 4 certainly will not behave egocentrically as Piaget would have predicted. If they are asked to say what a child who hasn't seen inside the box will think it contains, they will plump for candy. The 3-year-olds may be less sure but the 4-year-olds will be quite confident in attributing a different belief to other children. They can guess what other minds will think. (Even understanding the instructions in these studies requires some grasp of the issues; few researchers report that the toddlers got distressed or confused or just clammed up.)

Studies have found that 4-year-olds can also use information about what a character desires to predict whether he or she will be happy or sad or angry. These are all sophisticated judgements.

There has been a tendency for psychologists to find sophisticated behaviours younger and younger. Repacholi and Gopnik (1997) had 18-month-old toddlers taste two snacks – broccoli and goldfish crackers. Then an adult tasted each snack. To one snack the adult responded 'Mm' as in 'yummy', 'good'; to the other snack, the adult responded with a wry face and 'eww' nearly as in 'yuck'. In a match condition the adult liked the goldfish and disliked the broccoli like most 18-month-olds; in the mismatch, the adult liked the broccoli and disliked the crackers. When the adult then held her hand halfway between the two snacks and said, 'I want some more; can you give me some more?', the 18-month-old subjects overwhelmingly gave the adult more of what she, the adult, had liked. In the mismatch condition when the adult liked the broccoli, this meant the child understood that the adult preferred the vegetable to the snack the infant had liked. These were toddlers with insight. The only difficulty with this study is that the children may have been cued to produce these responses inadvertently like animals can be.

In studying how children understand pretending, we get a similar picture. Harris, Kavanaugh and colleagues have recently studied the development of how children understand pretending from the age of 17 months to 57 months. Harris and Kavanaugh have reported instances of children understanding pretending as early as 18 months. These infants, they found, responded to a request based on make-believe stipulations and behaved differently towards the same prop depending on what a scenario said it was.

In my Ph.D. thesis I reported a number of instances of similar abilities in one of my own children. The earliest pretence I saw was when one of my sons ran around the living room yelling 'I'm Batman' and draping a cape round his shoulders. He was 18 months old.

In a later study Kavanaugh and Harris found that 29-month-old children could understand what they called the pretend framework. If they gave children pretend changes, they could get in the spirit of the act. If, for example, the experimenters poured pretend tea over a duck, children aged 29 to 30 months were able to say that the duck was wet. In fact, no tea had been poured; the duck was as dry as before. Yet the children, in a spectacular refutation of Piaget's dictum that they are bound by their immediate perceptions, said the duck was now wet.

Older children (aged 36 months) were shown a puppet. The puppet poured pretend cereal into a bowl and then pretended to feed it to toy animals. Children could also impute pretend actions to a doll. This series of studies suggests that young children develop a considerable understanding of the grammar of pretending by the time they are 4.

In my thesis I reported a nicely sensitive example of that from a playschool I observed. The children sometimes showed they had an idea what others might think. Gabriel went into the Wendy House where Caroline was cuddling a baby doll. At 4 Gabriel knew babies might not like some things so he mimed a kiss. 'I only pretend to kiss your baby because he doesn't like kissing,' he announced. Caroline told him the baby wanted a kiss. Gabriel shook his head and wandered off.

Getting away with laughter

There is also evidence that children aged 2 to 3 years know their parents well enough to know that they might be able to get away with bad behaviour if they make them laugh. The British psychologist James Sully (1912) noted a number of instances in which his boy, aged 2 years 1 month, tried to get away with bad behaviour by laughing. The young Sully 'began to show himself a veritable rebel against parental authority'. He would sometimes hit his parents and 'follow up the sacrilege with a profane laugh'.

I observed many similar behaviours when I was doing my Ph.D. thesis. These are a set of notes from that time.

When N is 3.9 he knows it is time to go to bed. 'I won't,' he says and laughs at me. We go into his room and he deliberately puts his pyjama top the wrong way round. He laughs and then puts his trousers on and spins round like a top. 'Stop it,' I say. 'It's funny,' he insists. N also often laughed when annoying me by putting coins in his mouth, brushing his brother's toes with his toothbrush and other perverse, assertive acts of behaviour. He's convinced that if he laughs and, in particular, if he succeeds in making me laugh (as I sometimes do when he brushes his brother's feet with the toothbrush), he'll get away with it.

My sons may not have been able to explain what they were doing – yet they were doing it. Their actions suggest that even at the age of 3, they were able to calculate how other people might respond if they could make them laugh. This seems to be a sign of considerable social intelligence.

In the playgroup I also observed a different form of social intelligence. Sam, Giles and Robert (all 4 years old) are in the Wendy House out of sight. Sam: 'Shall we be dead and you be the doctor?' Sam and Giles lie down. Sam takes his pants off. Robert, the doctor, gets hold of the toy iron. He starts to iron Sam's bottom. Then he irons Sam's front. The children are completely quiet. Robert and Giles now also take their clothes off. Giles gets the iron and irons the others' bottoms.

They become very quiet when they realise the grown-ups who run the nursery are outside. They're socially smart enough at 4 to know they shouldn't be ironing each others' bottoms – and have sufficient insight into the adult mind to keep very mum about it.

Cutting and Dunn (1999) warn, however, that much of the research has been on middle-class and upper-middle-class children. They point out that there is a link between verbal ability and success on the false belief task. They also suggest that working-class children develop these skills a little later.

All this research begs the question of how much children guess about what adults are thinking. That's a game one can play with them.

The development of a theory of other minds

The theory that Bartsch and Wellman put forward describes three different stages. These stages are different from Piaget's but they approach cognitive development in a different light. Admitting that their data does only come from 10 children, only one of whom is African American, they nevertheless suggest a progression:

Before the age of 2 children do not generally use the language of 'I wish' and 'I desire' or 'I want'. At 2 years they often speak of wanting but they very rarely refer to thoughts and beliefs.

By the age of 3, children are much more likely to talk of thoughts.

By the age of 4 they are likely to talk of how other people think and feel and to use that as part of the explanation for action. The huge implication of this is that 4-year-olds are well on the way to being able to see things from the perspective of others. Piaget's and Vygotsky's theories never even considered such a possibility.

Bartsch and Wellman did not do experiments but analysed long samples of conversation. They did not – and it is not possible to – rule out alternative explanations for the patterns they identified. Their theory is a plausible narrative and has to be judged as that. It also has to be said that Siegler's overlapping waves model may apply especially to children as they develop a theory of mind. Any parent knows how infuriating toddlers can be, their behaviour changing from that of 2-year-olds who cry when they don't get their way to that of a super mature 5-year-olds who feel quite comfortable in giving you their view of the world.

Bartsch and Wellman also admit their data runs out after children are 5½ years old. They know perfectly well that children carry on developing ideas about the mind after that age so their theory is incomplete. It explains dramatic developments between 2 and 6 but it does not explain behaviour at other ages and stages. Wellman and Lagattuta (2000) in a later review are more bullish and state that 3-year-olds show 'a burgeoning mental construal of persons. Even as toddlers children go beyond external appearances and overt behavioural movements to consider the intentions, desires and emotions that underlie and cause overt action and expression' (p. 27).

Yet there are limits. Mercifully, while there is a long history of child prodigies in music, maths and even English, we have yet to have revealed unto us the pre-teen Freud. Despite their linguistic skills, Flavell and Wellman (1997) find that pre-school children, under 6 in America, find it hard to introspect. They get confused if asked to report their own feelings. They can use the language of feelings but they cannot really report perceptively on their own emotions. After the age of 6 that changes. Flavell *et al.* (1998) have more recently found that it is not till the age of 8 that children have much sense of being unconscious and that when you are asleep or unconscious, you cannot be aware of stimuli. Thankfully, even the 9-year-old child still has something to learn about how the mind works. Flavell and his co-workers (1998) presented children with stories whose heroes and heroines couldn't stop being plagued by certain thoughts. They asked questions about what they should do. Five-year-olds believed it was easily possible to stop thinking about things they didn't want to;

12-year-olds understood perfectly well that we can't totally control what thoughts we have. The 9-year-olds fell somewhere in between.

But while these findings remind us not to attribute too many skills to children, the thrust of the evidence is clear. By the age of 4, children do understand other people have thoughts of their own, different, individual ones.

Children and motives

Much of the research I have described has come from researchers like Wellman, Harris and Flavell who have been well aware of each other's work and been influenced by it. A Russian psychologist Subbotsky (1996) who is outside this group suggests children develop psychological theories about their own behaviour and that of others from the age of 4. Subbotsky engaged in complex dialogues with children, asking them questions such as whether newborns would be able to tell the difference between the smell of perfume and of rotten potatoes and whether babies could decide to perform certain actions.

By the age of 9, children offer reasons and motives which are very similar to those adults give. We have, therefore, a curious development. Piaget is almost certainly wrong in seeing children as advancing towards total logical maturity but children develop a psychological maturity that is unexpected between the ages of 6 and 9. I shall argue that exposure to a stream of soaps and dramas on television assists in this process.

It could be plausibly argued that this increasing psychological awareness is a cultural development that reflects the extent to which modern media report news in a psychological framework.

It's possible to review all these themes by looking at an ambitious attempt to marry Piaget's ideas with those of advocates of social and emotional intelligence.

The work of Case

Case and Yakamoto (1996) suggest it is possible to see connections between the ways in which children develop understanding of logical and mathematical concepts and the ways in which they develop social intelligence. In other words, a modified stage theory might handle the criticism that Piaget is too logical by proving children develop social and psychological thinking also in stages much like Piaget's four stages.

Case and his co-workers focus a great deal on how children understand numbers. They point out that 3- to 4-year-olds have two schemas for dealing with numbers. They can distinguish between quantities in a general way so they can tell the difference between *a little* and *a lot* of objects. They are also capable – and Case sees this as a second schema – of counting up to at least four or six. Case refers to this stage as Level 1.

Case suggests that round the age of 6, these two different schemas merge so that children develop what he calls 'a mental number line' which involves knowledge of number words – i.e. they know what 'eight' means; knowledge of written numbers – i.e. they know what '8' represents; a pointing routine so the child can tag objects while counting them; and a knowledge of cardinal set values.

Case argues that at age 4 children also use two separate schemas. On the one hand, they can use verbs such as 'I want' and 'I think' correctly. On the other hand, they can tell or follow a story in simple narrative steps. So the child can say 'The king went into the palace and then the King looked for his son.' But children can't bring these two schemas together. So they will not be able to make up or really follow a script which says that the king was worried about whether his son was frightened of him and hiding and that's why he went into the palace because he wanted to tell him he really loved him.

Around the age of 6, just as the number schemas merge, the story schemas merge so that children can relate events to motives, attributing intentions in an adult and understandable way. This is Level 2 thinking.

Case has suggested in total there are four stages in the development of cognitive competence across social, spatial and logical skills.

Case argues that at Level 1 the child can handle two sets of relations but does not see the connections between them. This shows itself in the way that the child deals with number, narrative and spatial concepts. As far as *number* is concerned the child can i. distinguish a lot from a little and ii. can also count. In *narrative terms*, the Level 1 child can i. talk of mental states and ii. can also tell stories where one event follows another, but he or she cannot deal with the causes of behaviour. In *spatial* terms the child can i. point out shapes and ii. can locate objects.

When the child reaches Level 2, the child can combine skills i. and ii. in all the domains above. For example, the child can count 8 objects and say whether in that particular context that counts for a lot or a little. Case argues that there is a major qualitative shift in thinking between the age of 5 and 7 allowing children as the child masters more complex relational structures. It is after the age of 7 however that children can understand two dimensions, as Case puts it. This is Level 3.

The Level 3 child can grasp more sophisticated combinations such as two story lines in a narrative and how these two narratives are related. At this stage the child can also understand how the actions of two characters may be related. In spatial terms, Case claims, this is when children begin to understand maps and perspective for the first time. By the age of 11, the child has started to develop real adult thinking which constitutes Level 4.

Case maintains that 'the view of the young child that has under-pinned the present theory has been that of a problem solver'. He says that his views are not 'an alternative to the previous views' – of Piaget and Vygotsky among others – but are 'a way of integrating them.' He allows far more influence than Piaget did to culture as 'contributing a vital set of tools to the child's repertoire.' Case wants education to provide 'activities which will maximise the chance that each individual child will be able to engage in some task that is appropriate for his or her current structural level on one hand and yet be able to progress towards higher levels on the other.' (p. 393, 1985)

Case is Piagetian in his faith in structure and stages but revisionist and so neo-Piagetian in that he thinks culture, teachers, and parents are vital in cognitive development. Case started work on his theory in the mid 1970s; his ideas on children failing to grasp two narratives till they are close to 7 years old should be set against Kinder's work on media literate toddlers who seem able to grasp two story lines, irony and other postmodern devices much earlier in life. This is examined in Chapter 10.

Case's ambitious work is far from finished. He has become the most influential of the neo-Piagetians. It is hard to know how to link his work with studies of brain imaging reported by Uta Frith (1999). She reports a number of studies where subjects were asked to either read or listen to stories which had a strong mental theme to them – stories about beliefs and promises. Subjects who listened to these stories seemed to have far more activity in a particular part of the frontal lobe. The brain, Frith suggests, has distinctive areas that deal with this kind of psychological material. The studies are of adults and so there is no information as yet on when children start to show such a pattern of brain activity.

Case's work also may not answer either the general critique of stage theories developed by Siegler (1996) or the more specific recent developments such as Subbotsky's work on the psychological insights of children.

Conclusion

Children become aware of other minds in stages that have some parallels with Piaget's ideas but the facts also suggest they are less egocentric than he said. Any proper account of cognitive development must not ignore social and emotional intelligence. It also can't ignore the paradox that children may become psychologically mature – surprisingly well-versed in emotional and psychological thinking – earlier and more easily than they become logically mature.

This is hypothetical but, if you were to ask teenagers the following questions:

(a) if they can tell you what it means to have a complex,
(b) how a child who has been sexually abused is likely to feel or whether that child is likely to tell on his abuser if the abuser is a member of his family,
(c) what a syllogism is,

I would guess many teenagers would give reasonable answers to (a) and (b) but few would do so to (c). Today's teenagers are likely to know more about psychology than about logic. Theories of development lag behind these trends all too often.

If you have or know teenagers, you can turn my hypotheticals into a test. I would love to know the results. You can send them to me at pysychologynews@lycos.co.uk.

Thinking matter

What are the implications of this for a general theory of cognitive development?

Consider the critique of the critique – If Piaget's theory focuses too much on logic, does this kind of work focus too much on simply observing children talk about certain issues?

Further reading

Bartsch K. and Wellman H. (1995) *Children Talk about the Mind*, Oxford University Press.

Siegler R.S. (1996) *Emerging Minds*, Oxford University Press.

Subbotsky E. (1996) *The Child as a Cartesian Thinker*, Hove, UK: Psychology Press.

6

The development of memory

Both very young and very old people are defective in memory,
the former because of growth, the latter owing to decay.
(Aristotle)

As so often, the Greek philosopher Aristotle set the tone for the
discussion 2,500 years ago. It used to be assumed that infant brains
were far too immature to remember anything at all. Piaget argued the
newborn could recall nothing because he lacked the cognitive structures
required.

In this chapter I look at:

- **childhood amnesia – do we forget most of our early childhood
  and why?**
- **what small babies can remember**
- **different memory skills at different ages in childhood**
- **how memories make up our identity.**

Yet some philosophers were well aware young children could
remember and could be encouraged to do so. John Locke admired the
ancient Jewish tradition of teaching children letters of the Hebrew
alphabet by baking little sweets in the shapes of letters (Locke 1702).
When a small child could recall the name and sound of a letter, he was

allowed to eat it. But Locke's gentle methods did not win much favour with teachers in the eighteenth, nineteenth or twentieth centuries. All too often teachers made their lack of confidence in children's ability to remember very clear.

In this chapter I write a good deal about my own personal memories. I hope this isn't ego. It's important to understand the growing academic research but it's also important to see the relationship between one's memories and one's sense of identity. Psychologists have become more formally interested in that with the growth of studies of autobiographical memory. Memories make us what we are. I am what I remember. I am what other people remember of me and it all starts in childhood.

I'll thump you into learning

When I was 10, I went to a very posh prep school in London. Our Latin master believed that the only way to get us to remember Latin verbs was to beat us with a bat if we failed to do so. The maths master threw lighted matches at us if we did not remember our tables. These 1950s teachers may seem eccentric but their techniques assumed what was the conventional psychological wisdom of the time. Only the fear of God – and the bat on the behind – would force lazy children to remember. Today, any teacher who adopted such techniques would find himself out of work and, in all probability, in court. Our teachers may have had a touch of the sadist about them but their notions of children's memories chimed well with contemporary psychological theories. Children had the capacity neither to store nor to retrieve memories very effectively. The methodological problem is that before children can speak, it requires considerable inventiveness to study whether children remember at all.

There have been many clever studies, however, which seem to show young children have unexpectedly good memories. The work of Rovee-Collier at Rutgers University, in particular, has consistently pushed back the frontiers. In one of her recent papers, she claims that by the age of 3 months, babies already have two memory systems functioning just as adults do (Gerhardstein, Adler and Rovee-Collier 1999). Rovee-Collier's work has provoked controversy and, also, as she is dealing with such young infants, she does not tackle an important aspect of recent work – the extent to which children's memories can be all too easily influenced by adults.

Sea slugs also remember

Organisms need less of a brain than used to be imagined to have functioning memory. The humble sea slug has some memory, it seems. Sea slugs do not have a brain and their nerve cells are distributed in ganglia – some of which are very large, being a millimetre in diameter. Eric Kandel of New York (who shared the Nobel Prize for Medicine in 2000) has studied the nerve cells crucial in habituation. If a slug is touched, it has a withdrawal reflex. If it is touched time and time again, that reflex diminishes. If it is touched with a noxious substance, the reflex reasserts itself. It 'remembers' it ought to withdraw which is, Kandel suggests, the most primitive form of memory. Kandel's work, of course, makes it seem more possible that tiny babies with as yet 'unformed' brains can remember.

Kandel has shown there are two key biochemical steps involved in sea slug memory. The first involves the neurotransmitter serotonin; the second involves calcium ions – ions are electrically charged particles – and calcium plays a large part in memory. When more calcium ions are released into the synapse, they affect synaptic connectivity, how easily the synapse fires. Biochemically, memories involve certain networks of synapses firing more easily. When you remember what it was like being told off by your English teacher and you can picture her face scowling at you, a network of synapses fires in your brain. The more easily that network fires, the easier it is for you to retrieve that 'being told off' memory.

Defining memory

Psychologists have defined memories in two very different ways – first, according to the length of time we have them and, second, according to the kinds of memories they are. The definitions by time are as follows.

Short-term memory – these are memories that last for a relatively short period. If I can remember the phone number you have just given me long enough to dial you back, my short-term memory is in good shape. Psychologists disagree on how long short-term memory lasts. Some claim it is mere seconds and that there is a **sensory store** even before short-term memory. Others claim short-term memory lasts a matter of minutes. From the developmental point of view, the crucial question is when and how infants develop short-term memory.

Working memory – working memory is a highly influential theory devised by Professor Alan Baddeley of Bristol University and Graham Hitch (Baddeley 1997). Baddeley claims working memory is longer than short-term memory but shorter than long-term memory. The main components of working memory are an **articulatory loop** in which words and sounds are stored for up to two seconds and the **visuo-spatial sketchpad** which stores and manipulates images for again a matter of seconds. Both work together with the **central executive** which uses information from the loop and the sketchpad to reason or to provide solutions to problems. The executive acts on these verbal and visual flickers of memory to produce actions. From the developmental point of view, the key question is again when these three components start to function.

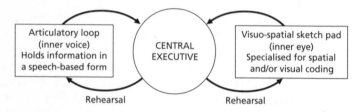

The Baddeley and Hitch (1997) model of working memory.

No one has really solved the problem of how short-term memories become long-term memories and whether this involves one process or a number of processes – and what the biochemistry of these processes might be. Rehearsing memories clearly plays a part. By rehearsing a memory, psychologists mean repeating it. I have had, since the age of 10, vivid images of the maths teacher flinging lighted matches at members of the class. I have talked about these memories, seen them in my mind's eye a number of times. Everyone suspects that rehearsing short-term memories transfers them into long-term memory. But how does that happen?

Long-term memory – these are the memories of events in the distant past. So called autobiographical memories, memories of events in one's own life, are inevitably long-term memories. These memories are being investigated more than ever before.

Exercise

Write down what you think are your earliest memories. What age do you think you were when you experienced the events? Talk to your own parents to see how accurate your recollection is. (This assumes your parents will remember correctly which has its own risks but there are few perfect ways of checking.) Focus on that earliest memory. Just how much detail can you recall?

It is likely you will not have a flood of memories.

Childhood amnesia: the mystery of memory

Old people can sometimes remember very early incidents in their lives. In 1992, the Nobel Prize winner Sir John Eccles told me he could remember a day in the Australian outback 88 years earlier when he had to leave home quickly. He was not quite 3 years old. He and his father had met the local doctor riding towards their house. Eccles knew why the memory was so well lodged in his mind. It turned out to be the day his sister was born.

Eccles' experience reinforces the idea that important memories are memories which have some sort of emotion attached to them; his sister's birth was a very significant family event. Also, people do tend to remember their first kiss. But Eccles had also often rehearsed this memory of the ride in the outback, he told me. The initial emotional impact as well as the recurring rehearsal had made it one of those scenes from his life that he could always easily retrieve and see in his mind's eye, even though it was 88 years since the event.

When I asked Eccles if he remembered many other events from when he was 3, he said no. And in this he was typical. One of the curious facts of memory is that we remember very little from our early childhood. Some psychologists think this is because the memory traces that are laid down so early in life are not very stable and decay; others believe that the memories are somewhere in the brain but hard to retrieve.

Everyone accepts, however, that we forget most of our early childhood. A study by Henri and Binet over a hundred years ago asked 123 adults to name their first memories (Henri and Binet 1896) and not one could recall anything from when he was 2 years or younger. Pillemer and White (1989) found that on average the earliest memory adults had was of events when they were 3½ years old.

For most of us, our earliest memory is of an event that happened when we were 3 years old. Copyright © Popperfoto.

In an informal study I carried out for the Channel 4 science series *Equinox*, we asked 30 people what their first memories were and how old they thought they were when the event had happened. One man remembered his parents fighting; one woman, being splashed with water on a summer outing; one man, a professor of psychology, remembered getting a beautiful red truck when he was 3. There was no particular pattern to these memories.

But these early memories may not be accurate. In his autobiography Piaget wrote that he had been convinced for a long time that he had been kidnapped when he was very young. He repeatedly told people of this experience only to discover from his nursemaid that it was a fantasy.

Most of the first memories reported in the Channel 4 study, like Eccles' memory, were of single events. They did not fit into a particular pattern. Usually, we have connected memories so that you can summon up and link images that will tell you, for example, what it was like to live in a particular place or to describe, say, a birthday party or the journey to school – only from later in childhood, from around the age of 8 or 9. I have little difficulty in summoning up many scenes of my life in the London prep school I attended but then I was 10 years old by the time I got there. Early memories are rarer and more fragmented.

Sigmund Freud developed an intriguing theory to explain what he called childhood amnesia – or forgetting most events from childhood. Freud argued childhood amnesia is the result of the distressing psychological conflicts the child faces. Freud claimed young boys have an Oedipus complex and young girls have an Electra complex. Very crudely, Freud claimed the young boy hates his father and wants to replace him, so that his mother will love only him; the young girl hates her mother and wants to replace her, so that she will have her father's undivided attention. These fierce sexual wishes are partly conscious, partly unconscious. By the age of 3 or 4, the child knows that they are both hopeless and sinful. So the child represses many of the feelings and memories involved.

Eventually, according to Freud, the boy resolves the Oedipus complex by identifying with his father and the girl resolves the Electra complex by identifying with her mother. But this process is so painful that feelings and desires have to be censored and driven into the unconscious. As a result of these powerful conflicts, those childhood memories are suppressed, repressed, depressed.

One psychologist who argues she has evidence that fits Freud's theory is Kathleen Nelson. She taped the babblings of a toddler called Emily from when Emily was 16 months old. When her parents were not in the room – and Emily thought she was alone – her words reflected a good deal of anxiety and emotion. When her parents were visible, she babbled less anxiously (Nelson 1989), proof perhaps that babies repress something. In his survey of the scientific evidence for and against Freud, the late Paul Kline reviewed the evidence for and against Freud's view of the causes of infantile amnesia and came down with a firm 'not proven but not totally out of the question' (Kline 1991). Kline stressed that alternative explanations of childhood amnesia, such as that we cannot retrieve these early traces either because they are so brittle they have decomposed, or because they are buried so deep in neural networks they cannot be accessed, are as unproved as Freud's ideas.

Certainly, any account of the development of memory needs to explain why we remember so little of our early life – and also why old people often start to remember images of their youth and childhood. Or are these images pure fantasy?

Different types of memory again

Time, which divides memories into short-term, long-term, is not the only way of dividing memories. Psychologists also refer to: **episodic memory** – the remembering of particular episodes or scenes such as that last night you went to the Venue and the band playing were Goatbag; **semantic memory** – remembering rules, definitions and words. Our semantic memory is our store of facts about the world. The facts that the sky is usually blue, that 'fractious' means brittle or quarrelsome and that Henry VIII had six wives are part of our semantic memory; **procedural memory** – remembering the correct sequences of a process, hence procedural. You cannot cook a hamburger without remembering that you have to buy meat, make it into a pattie, switch the cooker on, etc.; **prospective memory** – remembering not the past but making plans for the future. I remember now that I have to meet Jackie tomorrow at 6; **implicit memory** – sometimes a person is not aware of particular facts or events they can recall when they are prompted to do so. The term also can cover buried memories we're not conscious of. One example would be recalling that one had been sexually abused as a child many years later – a topic that generates much controversy. Tests of implicit memory often ask subjects to identify rather than to remember something but that identification will depend on memory. As a result there are disputes about the nature of implicit memory. In their magisterial *Handbook of Human Memory* (2000) Tulving and Craik note that some researchers claim, for example, remembering Paris is the capital of France can be an implicit memory; **explicit memory** – these memories are conscious, easily accessible memories. Tests for this are simpler because subjects are simply asked if they remember who won the Triple Jump in the Sydney Olympics; **flashbulb memory** – so called because psychologists have found that people have a kind of photograph of where they were and what they were doing at the moment when they learned of some momentous event. In November 1963, I was 15 and watching television with my mother and one of her friends, Lotte Steiner, when we heard on the television that President Kennedy had been shot dead. For British people, other key events will tend to be the fall of Mrs Thatcher and the death of Princess Diana. These memories seem to act as book-marks.

These different kinds of memory underline the complexity of the process. Psychologists and physiologists have also spent much of the last thirty years trying to work out the chemical and electrical changes which must happen in the brain to lay down long-term memory traces. The questions for developmental psychologists have tended to be basic – at what age do children remember what kind of information? What is the relationship between age and the accuracy of recall? How does the short-term memory of children differ from that of adults, if it does?

The study of memory in childhood is also complicated by the fact that it overlaps learning so much. Human beings have such a long childhood because we have to learn so much before we can function as adults. Today's children have to learn to read, to write, to do maths, social skills, sexual skills and much else beside. But the latest evidence is that our ability to learn and to remember starts while we are in the womb.

Does memory start in the womb?

Some of the most fascinating recent research has shown that foetuses have some sort of memory capacity. From the neurological point of view that is perhaps not surprising.

It is not just the miserable sea slug which remembers more than we once imagined. Work by Peter Hepper (1991) in Belfast shows that while they are still in their mothers' womb, babies notice the signature tunes of television programmes such as *Neighbours*. And when they are born, they will respond more to that tune than to other pieces of music. Whatever one may think of the TV serial, this is an impressive demonstration of the fact that our memory system starts to work even before we are born. For the foetus must have been able to store the memory of the *Neighbours* tune and, then, be able to access and retrieve it.

As surprising perhaps are studies which show newborn babies are capable of some form of imitation from the first moments of their life. To imitate you sticking your tongue out, the baby has to remember that someone stuck a tongue out and to have some mechanism that allows them to make their muscles replay the action.

Imitation may require some sort of memory capacity but it is not memory as we normally understand it. The most compelling evidence for the memory of babies comes from a series of studies by Carolyn Rovee-Collier at Rutgers University. In the early 1990s, she started a series of experiments with infants of 8 weeks and older. Her work is an example of the way psychologists have to be creative when trying to study the abilities of babies because they can't speak.

If a toddler sees a toy, he or she can whoop 'there again'. The baby cannot make such meaningful sounds but Rovee-Collier argues the baby will show motor signs of excitement. She uses the rate at which babies kick in response to a mobile to establish whether or not they remember. The logic is simple. If babies remember nothing, then it will not matter to them what mobile they look at. But if they do remember, one should be able to find motor signs of that memory. First, the babies are trained to kick when they see a mobile. A baseline for the kicking of each baby is established. Later, the babies are tested with a mobile that either displays the same stimuli or different ones from the training mobile. The rate of kicking 'tells' Rovee-Collier whether the babies 'remember' the stimulus as the same they saw earlier. If they kick more than their baseline, then that is 'yes, the same' but if they do not kick above the baseline, then the babies are saying no. The logic of this can be debated but Rovee-Collier has got impressively consistent results over a decade.

Rovee-Collier found that if one trains babies to kick when they see a mobile, they will kick more when they see a familiar mobile than when they see a new one. This only makes sense if they have a memory of some mobiles. She claims babies as young as 8 weeks will kick far more at a mobile they have seen before than at a new mobile. When 3-month-olds are tested by being shown the mobile they were trained on, they show near perfect retention for several days after training. To a new mobile, the 3-month-olds kick much less.

Later work by Rovee-Collier looked at 24 6-month-old babies. They were presented with mobiles in a specific order. Again the measure of whether they recognised anything was their rate of kicking. One of the best-known laws of adult memory is that if you present subjects with a list of 5 or 13 stimuli, they will tend to remember the first one presented better than the rest. This is called the primacy effect. Rovee-Collier found that when the 24 babies were presented with 3 different mobiles, there was evidence the one shown to them first was

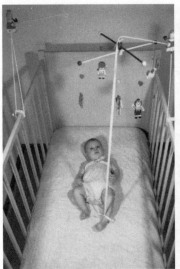

Carolyn Rovee-Collier uses rate of kicking in response to stimuli to study memory in babies. Reprinted with permission from C.K. Rovee-Collier, M.W. Sullivan, M. Enright, D. Lucas, and J.W. Fagan (1980), Reactivation of infant memory. *Science, 208*, 1159–1161. Copyright © 1980 American Association for the Advancement of Science. Courtesy of Carolyn Rovee-Collier.

remembered best. The memory of the 6-month-olds was already organised in such a way that they showed the primacy effect. The effect disappeared, however, when the babies were presented with 5 mobiles. The study suggests that by the age of 6 months, babies' memories are starting to work along the same lines as adult memory systems. The memory capacity of babies is much smaller so when there are 5 mobiles there is too much information for them to handle, but with 3 mobiles, the laws of adult memory apply.

In her latest studies, Rovee-Collier asked whether 3-month-old infants possess two memory systems for objects as adults do – one that is sensitive to the size of objects. They were trained with a mobile on which an S was marked. Twenty hours later, the babies were presented either with a mobile with the same S or with an S that was either 33 per cent larger or smaller. The babies in the no size change condition kicked well above baseline proving, given Rovee-Collier's model, that they had remembered the S.

In a second study, Rovee-Collier looked at the effects of priming, in effect, preparing a subject for a new stimulus. Thirty three-month-olds were tested. First, they were trained to kick to a mobile with the S. Two weeks later, they were tested just as the babies in the first experiment were tested. But the day before this test, the infants had been 'primed'. The experimenter showed them the mobile they had seen two weeks earlier but it was the experimenter who moved it about. The priming stimulus had the original S, not the S that was either 33 per cent larger or 33 per cent smaller than before. Infants now seemed to kick significantly above the baseline level when, the day after the priming, they were shown a mobile with the original S, or the larger S or the smaller S. She claims to have proved 3-month-olds have two memory systems operating – one that only works for stimuli that are identical in size to the one first shown and one that is size insensitive, where the size does not matter. This is again similar to adult memory. Rovee-Collier complains, however, that 'developmental and cognitive psychologists have resisted conclusions that infants have two functionally distinct memory systems (Gerhardstein, Adler and Rovee-Collier 2000).

Your face? I remember it well

There are problems with Rovee-Collier's work. It does make large assumptions in relating rate of kicking to memory. It also must be said that mobiles are not a naturally occurring phenomenon and one might expect a baby's first memories to be for stimuli that were crucial to them – faces. The baby needs to recognise the faces of his or her mother, father and significant others. Charles Nelson of the University of Minnesota has shown that 6-month-old babies can remember faces. Bartrip, Morton and de Schonen (2001) have shown that 5-week-old babies can recognise their mothers from just features like the mouth and nose. How they manage is not clear but again infantile memory is at work. Nelson placed electrodes on the scalps of the babies and found that the patterns of response from the visual cortex triggered by familiar faces differ from those of unfamiliar faces (Nelson 1995).

Another impressive demonstration of the recall ability of babies comes from McDonough (1999). In Chapter 2, we examined in some detail Piaget's ideas on object permanence. Piaget did not see object permanence as an exercise in memory but McDonough argues that it can be seen in that light. To know that an object is permanent means you have to remember that it existed before the experimenter hid it. McDonough tested 28 babies who were on average 7 months 14 days old.

First, the experimenter showed the infant two boxes. Both were empty. Then, the experimenter handed an object to the baby who was allowed to handle it. Then, the experimenter took the object back from the child. Then, the object was placed in one of the boxes. The baby saw which box the object was placed in but the object was hidden from view. In other words, the child had to remember that the object existed. The experimenter then interacted with the child by playing with its fingers. Then after one minute of such distraction the experimenter jiggled both boxes in front of the baby.

The measure of what the child remembered was seeing which of the boxes it reached for. Fifteen of the 28 babies reached more towards the box where the object was placed. (The scientists claimed this was significant.) The study looked at 3 different conditions and the babies did worse when they were picked up and carried round the room. These findings reinforce Piaget's ideas that children develop schemas round the age of 8 months – and these schemas are lodged in the brain and can be recalled.

If, by the age of 8 months, babies can remember stimuli such as mobiles, faces and where objects are placed, what is the next step?

By the age of eleven months

By the age of 11 months infants can reproduce very simple sequences in an experimental session. If they see a donkey doll being pulled on a string, for example, they can repeat the action or imitate it. By 18 months, they can certainly repeat the action even if they last saw it performed a week earlier. Between 12 and 24 months, many babies start to babble, to point and even to speak. Both pointing and speaking obviously help in the development of memory. It has been argued that speaking alters the nature of memory because the child can now share his or her memories with others.

One of the difficulties with studies of childhood memory is that psychologists often compare a group of 12-month-olds with a group of 24-month-olds. One gets snapshots of memory at these two different ages rather than a sense of the progress children make. One exception is the work of Robyn Fivush who has carried out a longitudinal study of the same 19 children over a 30-month period. The children were aged 3 years 4 months when the study started. They were then re-tested when they were 3 years 10 months, 4 years 10 months and 5 years 10 months. The tests included asking them questions about events that they had personally experienced. Fivush built up a catalogue of the children's experiences so they could be asked at 4 years and 10 months not just about a recent event but about an event they had been asked about a year earlier (Fivush 1998).

Fivush found that 72 per cent of children aged 3 years 10 months could recall an event from six months previously quite accurately. In this she confirmed the findings of Ceci described in Chapter 4. Three-year-olds certainly have effective longer-term memories. Fivush also claims that children organise memories in ways that do not seem intuitively strange to adults. She found that these were the main organising headings:

activities – a child will say 'I ran to school'
objects – there were balloons in the playground
persons – my mother cooked roast beef
locations – we went to visit the museum
descriptives – the sun was setting over the river when we had a picnic
internal states – I felt happy when I got a present from my uncle.

The implications of Fivush's work are interesting. First, her work suggests it is reasonable to claim that by 3 years 10 months, children are aware of the fact that memories can be shared with others. Second, by the age of 4 children are starting to organise complex social material in recognisable ways.

At the same time there is evidence that children from the age of 4 become reasonably adept at recalling practical information. Friedman (1991) found that children aged 4, 6 and 8 could all remember, after 7 weeks, seeing a video on how to brush their teeth – and the hints it gave – though the younger ones were confused by how long it was since they had viewed. Curiously, however, children seem less good at remembering information on road safety though it is not entirely clear whether the problem is that young children don't have a clear concept of danger.

Parental exercises

The poet T.S. Eliot spoke of the evening with the 'photograph album'. I think this was an excellent Victorian and early twentieth-century invention. Now I suspect we take far more photographs than ever before but, paradoxically, we probably spend less time looking at them. I'm not suggesting that either teachers or parents should turn themselves into photo bores. 'Tonight is the night when we project my stills and I talk about them.' But pictures provide a wonderful aid to talking to children about common memories. You can, after all, follow Fivush and take photographs of your child's third birthday party and talk about the party and the people involved three weeks, three months and six months later. There is no research that proves what this will do but it probably will at least get the kids talking.

The ability to remember must be linked to what is the greatest learning feat of all human beings – learning to talk. By the age of 4 most children use the verb 'I remember' appropriately so they begin to have not just the use of their memories but the concept of memory. But this is a skill that develops only slowly and with errors being made.

Talking about memories

Flavell and Wellman (1997), in an important study, showed that children tended to overestimate their own memory and to ignore the kind of mnemonic tricks people use in order to recall things effectively. This study of so called metamemory was influential in backing up the idea that children had poor memories.

Few of the experiments I've described so far – Rovee-Collier's mobiles, recall of tooth brushing – deal with vital personal memories. Since the 1970s, however, the question of child abuse has become unavoidable. There has been a complex debate about the extent of abuse and so-called false memory syndrome. The literature is huge and very controversial. Much of it deals with whether adults can correctly recall instances of being abused twenty or more years before. There are over 36,000 children in the United Kingdom on child protection registers and 26 per cent of all rapes, according to the NSPCC are committed against children. In dealing with such allegations – often brought by one parent against another parent in the context of divorce proceedings

– it is important for police, social workers and judges to know whether or not children are remembering events accurately.

Stephen Ceci, professor of developmental psychology at Cornell University, has been a leading investigator in this area. His research makes him insist that adults need to be much more skilled in talking to children about their memories. Sensitively interviewed, children as young as 3 can have perfectly good memories of events that took place in the past.

'The most humbling thing is when I look at the interviews I've done. I know the mistakes one shouldn't make. I'm not aware of making them. Then when I look back at it on video, I find I'm making all the same mistakes,' Ceci told me.

In the 1980s, Ceci was already an expert on memory. One day he took a macabre phone call from a judge. A woman's body had been found concreted below her living room. Her sister claimed the woman had been killed by her husband. The key witness was the victim's son. The prosecution claimed the child recalled that when he was 4 he had seen his father hitting his mother with a baseball bat. 'The judge wanted to know if he could believe a child's memories of such an event,' Ceci told me, 'I was clueless.'

A little shamed, Ceci decided to focus on memories for more relevant events. He is now a key figure in the debate on how credible children are as witnesses. If Piaget is right and pre-operational children are tied to their immediate perceptions, 3-year-olds shouldn't have good memories because memories involve recalling what is not in front of you.

Ceci discovered the opposite is the truth. 'After ten years, I'm struck by how well children, as young as three, remember ordinary events,' Ceci said. Ninety-five per cent can describe accurately an event from three months previously. So how are they tied to the here and now?

'The problem is the adults who have access to children's memories,' Ceci said. Allegations of abuse oblige children to talk to social workers, police, lawyers, psychologists. Young children don't like to talk about embarrassing events. When embarrassed children won't talk, the silence worries the interviewers. The right technique, Ceci says, is to wait and gently prompt the child. Many interviewers hate the silence, and bombard the child with questions. It's this bombardment that confuses children especially as the questions asked are often very suggestive. The way questions are phrased influences not just what children say but what they come to believe. 'Suggestive' questions can trigger a child's imagination to create 'false beliefs'.

To test his hypothesis Ceci devised a series of experiments where children aged 3, 4 and 6 years had an unexpected visitor to their class-room, Sam Stone. He walked in, commented on the book that was being read and then walked out after 2 minutes. Normally children remember that nothing more happened.

'But if you start to seed things,'Ceci said, 'you can make children believe something very different happened.' Some children were told that Sam was clumsy and often broke things; others were questioned in ways which suggested there had been trouble when Sam was in class. The effect was dramatic. Seventy-two per cent of children then embellished their accounts of Sam's visit – some with many imagined details of his destructive behaviour.

Children can get so confused by this 'seeding' that they may well start to believe things that did not happen did happen. Ceci has found 35 per cent of 6-year-olds can develop such false beliefs.

Open-ended questions are the best way to combat bias. Ceci has found, however, that between 30 per cent and 35 per cent of questions used in interviews are closed – and many are suggestive.

It's also vital to check what children mean by their words. In one case a woman alerted the police when her 3-year-old daughter said that 'daddy put his pee-pee in my pee-pee'. Good interviewing unpicked a domestic reality. The girl had gone to the toilet, peed and not flushed; 'daddy' had gone to the bathroom later, peed and, inevitably, put his pee-pee into her pee-pee.

Distorted memories and the non-existent mousetrap

In another experiment Ceci got a 5-year-old boy to be asked questions about how he had gone into the basement of their house and found a mouse. The questions asked the boy how he had got his finger trapped in the mousetrap and what it was like to be taken to hospital. In reality, none of this had happened. There was no mouse, no mousetrap and no frantic rush to the hospital.

Ceci recorded the interview sessions on tape. After some weeks of questioning, the boy said he had been taken to the hospital because his finger hurt so much. He had developed what Ceci calls a false memory. This slightly fairy-tale study is important because Ceci believes it is very easy for well-meaning social workers and police officers to question children in an insistent way so that they remember incidents of child abuse that never happened.

Ceci is not suggesting child abuse never happens but just pleading for adults to understand that children can be very easily led to say they remember things that never, in fact, took place. This suggests children's memory traces are not as 'strong' as those of adults but neither psychologists nor biologists have any clear idea of the biochemical mechanisms that might be responsible. What is important is that adults who ask children to remember significant events should understand how easy it is to influence children's memories.

There is one final aspect of the development of memory to consider.

The teenage reminiscence bump

According to Martin Conway of Bristol University, a key change happens at around the age of 12 or 13. Our memories from our teenage years and up to the age of 25 are better than we have reason to expect. We can remember the recent past best but then there is what is called a reminiscence bump for years between 13 and 25. The reason, Conway argues, is linked to the ideas of the psychoanalyst Erik Erikson. Erikson argued that between these ages our sense of identity gels. However old we become, we tend to remember the things that happened to us then. Conway suggests that it is because in this period we have conscious formative experiences – the first date, the first kiss, the exam success that make the family proud, the realisation that we were never going to play football well enough to get a test for a real club, university, the first job. And so we remember these events better because they are the building blocks of our identity.

Conclusions

We have traced some of the important milestones in the development of memory. We have seen that even babies seem to have some ability to recall and that by the age of 3 years infants seem to have good recall as long as adults are willing to listen and do not butt in all the time, ask leading questions and, without knowing it, bend children's memories. This descriptive evidence is impressive. Physiological studies of adult memory are interesting and point to the importance of areas in the brain like the hippocampus and the amygdala in process-ing memory. Nevertheless, another confession of psychological ignorance, we still know little about how the underlying brain mechanisms develop in children.

Materials

A film of Ceci's work is available from *Psychology News*, 4 Newell St, London E14 7HR, price £14.95.

7

Measuring children's cognitive development

Introduction

Throughout this book I have tried to argue that psychology of children's cognitive development tends to lag behind events and that changes in the family and in the exposure of children to media are affecting aspects of their development. Since psychologists seek to establish fundamental laws of development, we tend to look for universal patterns. This is how children develop, have always developed and will always develop. That emphasis may make us miss interesting changes.

In this chapter I explore:

- **the origins of testing children's intelligence**

- **the nature of intelligence and whether IQ tests are adequate**

- **the nature of creativity**

- **how we measure intelligence.**

Human beings have valued intelligence since Biblical times. Plato and Aristotle have remained famous for 2,500 years because of their extraordinary intelligence. The education of children has been a major concern of most societies since Classical Greece. In Britain since the seventeenth century there have been influential texts on how to teach children and how to nurture their intelligence. The philosopher John

Locke's *Thoughts Concerning the Education of Children* written in 1702 is far from being the first text but it is one that was very influential.

Despite Locke, by the early twentieth century, the British seemed to have developed a curious attitude to intelligence. P.G. Wodehouse in his popular books written from 1910 on suggests that a proper gentleman has more bottom than brains. It is the butler Jeeves who has the perfectly oiled brain. The writer who caught this distrust of intelligence best perhaps was the Hungarian immigrant George Mikes who wrote a wonderful book *How to be an Alien*, a guide for immigrants to Britain. Mikes pointed out that Britain was the only country in the world to use a phrase like 'too clever by half'. In France, Hungary, Germany and the rest of the world the idea that you could be too intelligent is unknown. Currently, however, a senior British politician, David Willetts, is known as 'two brains'; his crime was to have a first from Oxford. Mikes astutely pointed out that in the heady days of the Empire, the British felt that they did not need extra brains to rule the world. Compare the ridicule poured on the less than alpha-brained Dan Quayle when he was Vice President!

These quaint attitudes have changed. Since the 1970s British politicians have been worried by the failure of many British children to learn to read, write and be numerate. A study by the Basic Skills Agency suggested that over 25 per cent of British teenagers have difficulties with basic literacy and numeracy. There is more pressure than ever before on children in British schools to do well, to show their intelligence and indeed they are being tested now from the age of 3.

A book on cognitive psychology has to grapple with the issue of how well we measure children's intelligence, whether those measurements miss out on important abilities such as creativity and innovation and whether intelligence is largely genetically determined or very much influenced by the environment. This is an ancient hot potato on which more progress has been made in the last twenty years than ever before.

Intelligence is not just, as we shall see, a matter of verbal and mathematical skills but those skills are key elements that make up all intelligence tests.

Despite valuing intelligence, the idea of measuring it didn't occur till around 1870, however.

Measuring intelligence is complex and there have been controversies between psychologists like Hans Eysenck (1979) and Paul Kline (1990), both now sadly dead, who argued IQ tests are the best method and others such as Howard Gardner and Robert Sternberg who see these IQ tests as too narrow.

Even Eysenck, a fan of IQ tests, admitted they did not predict future success too well (1995). He was acid about MENSA, the club for high IQ scorers that only admits those who score above 140. For many MENSA members, Eysenck noted, their biggest achievement was scoring high on IQ tests. MENSA members weren't specially rich, famous or happy. Personality factors, persistence, motivation and the ability to get on with other people mattered as much as raw intelligence in the game of life. These factors also affect how well children do on IQ tests.

Varieties of IQ test

IQ tests have a long history. In the 1881 exhibition the Victorian polymath Sir Francis Galton set up a stall in the Natural History Museum at South Kensington as part of the International Exhibition. For 3 old pennies you could have your intelligence scientifically measured as well as the size of your head.

Galton also devised a number of simple tests including tests of speed of reaction to stimuli. Eysenck has built on Galton's ideas to argue there is a simple definition – and explanation – of intelligence. It's essentially quickness of mind. Intelligent individuals, children and adults, process information more quickly from their early childhood on.

Norms of achievement

Twenty-three years after Galton's 1881 exhibition, two French psychologists Alfred Binet and Theodore Simon were commissioned by the city of Paris to examine the effectiveness of schools. The city wanted to provide extra help for children who were not doing well. Binet and Simon came up with the idea of measuring **norms of achievement** for different ages.

Binet and Simon looked at what most children of a particular age could achieve. They soon came up with lists of tasks that a normal 4-year-old child was able to perform. To modern psychologists, their lists are a quaint mix of tasks. Four- to 6-year-old children were given a set of instructions to follow. For one task, they were told to pick up a key, put it on a chair at one end of the room, shut a door, then pick up a box and bring it back to the experimenter. To succeed the child had to remember a sequence of five actions. That was beyond most 4-year-olds.

Half the 5-year-olds Binet and Simon tested, however, did manage the sequence. Through such exercises the researchers discovered norms. The average 6-year-olds could manage the following:

> distinguish between morning and evening
> copy the picture of a diamond
> count thirteen pennies
> distinguish between pictures of ugly and pretty faces.

The normal 8-year-old could manage to:

> compare two objects from memory
> count up to 20 without hesitation
> say what had been left out of a picture he had just seen
> repeat a list of 5 digits.

Binet and Simon's questions have many of the hallmarks of IQ tests. Seven of the eight questions have a clear right or wrong answer; the only one where there is room for debate is what's a pretty and an ugly face. Is what a Paris psychologist thinks of as a pretty face the universally correct answer? In the South Pacific they might have different ideas. Binet and Simon's questions also don't touch the question of children's creative or imaginative thinking.

Intelligence is a relative measure

As Binet and Simon discovered what was normal for children of different ages, they were able to quantify just how clever or not a particular child was in comparison with other children. The IQ test is a comparative measure, not an absolute one. If I weigh 62 kilos that is an absolute measure. I may be light or heavy for my age and height but the 62 kilos is 62 kilos.

IQ scores are different. They are relative scores, comparing a child with the average for his group – not absolute scores.

Binet and Simon's work led to the birth of the IQ which stands for **Intelligence Quotient**. You would give a child a series of 20 questions.

The psychologist knew the norm for 6-year-olds was to be able to answer 14 of these questions.

If a child got 14 out of the 20 questions right, he or she would have an IQ of 100, dead average. Simon and Binet's norms made it possible to work out what the child's mental age was. If an 8-year-old child could answer all 20 questions and that was normal for an 8-year-old, then his or her intelligence quotient was 125.

The intelligence quotient was this fraction:

Mental age/chronological age × 100.

With the 6-year-old child who answered all the questions an 8-year-old should, his IQ score would be:

8 divided by 6 = 1.25 × 100 = 125.

Research from 1903 to 1960 showed that only 4 children in 1,000 have an IQ of above 140. Einstein's IQ has been reckoned at above 180.

Binet and Simon's work focused on children but IQ testing was soon taken up by the American army who were interested in adults. During the 1914 war IQ tests were used on 1.75 million recruits. The huge amount of data generated encouraged researchers to study how fair the tests were and to improve their design. This led to the main IQ tests whose descendants are still in use: the Stanford Binet, the Wechsler and Raven's Matrices. But none of this answered the key question of what intelligence is.

What is intelligence?

We all know people who are good with words but hopeless with numbers. The absent-minded academic is a cliché but they exist. I once had a friend, Barry, who was an excellent psychologist and could debate the pros and cons of Piaget with the best. Nevertheless, Barry tended to leave things on the stove and cause fires. Once he burned two budgies he was very fond of to death. Good with words, good with numbers but as impractical as you could imagine.

Barry highlights one problem in measuring cognitive development. Is it a question of measuring intelligence or a number of different intelligences? I flatter myself I'm very good with words, not bad with numbers but I have a below average spatial sense and am musically inept. You could score my results on IQ or intelligence tests two ways:

Verbal intelligence 130

Numerical intelligence 120

Spatial intelligence 92

Musical intelligence 78

Report 1: Averaged out intelligence score 420/4 = 105 – just above average intelligence. Will do well in admin work.

The averaged out intelligence score suggests someone of very medium abilities. But if you analyse the scores differently, if you don't lump them together a very different profile emerges.

Report 2: High verbal score, good on maths, appalling at other tasks. Suggest journalism, advertising copywriter or maths teacher. On no account hire as architect or violinist.

Exercise in self-observation

Scoring yourself out of 10, put down where you think you rate at:

verbal ability

numerical ability

spatial ability

practical ability

musical ability

creativity

Be honest. Research suggests we rate ourselves a little flatteringly but most of us have quite a good grasp of our abilities.

The general factor of intelligence

At first psychologists were not sure whether they were testing one general intelligence or verbal, numerical, spatial and practical intelligences. In 1927, a series of statistical studies showed there was an underlying link to all these scores – a factor of general intelligence.

This factor called 'g' accounted for around 52 per cent of the variance – a statistical concept which essentially means the difference in the scores.

The argument seemed to have been decided once and for all. There was a g factor, a factor of general intelligence. Children either were intelligent or not. In Britain when children did the 11-plus to weed out those who would go to grammar schools and those who would go to less academic secondary moderns, an IQ test was an important part of the exam. Kline (1990) has argued that what IQ is best at predicting is educational achievement rather than success in later work.

The discovery of the g factor also had implications for the **nature v. nurture** argument. It strengthened the hand of those who believed that intelligence was largely inherited. Some fifty years later, a number of psychologists including Eysenck, claimed intelligence was largely inherited and that there was a simple biological difference between the clever and the slow. The use of the word 'slow' to describe less bright people was the wisdom of common speech. But the evidence is not that clear cut.

Intelligent children

To start with, history is full of great men and women who, as children, gave every impression of being not merely average but quite backward as in the case of Albert Einstein whose failure to speak early I mentioned earlier. Einstein's school career was not glittering and he failed a number of exams. Winston Churchill was considered a dunce at school. Disappointing his parents spurred the young Winston to prove himself clever and brave – and he published his first book in his early 20s to make a point.

Different tests of thinking

Given thinking is such a mix of operations, measuring children's cognitive development is complex. To do it properly requires a variety of tests. At the very least these include:

- tests of perception – can the child see, hear, speak properly? If they can't, you may never know their intelligence because they don't get the questions they are being asked;

- tests of problem-solving abilities – the typical questions IQ tests put. These only test one kind of thinking;
- tests of less problem-focused kinds of thinking – especially divergent and creative thinking.

Dissecting IQ tests

IQ tests only measure one style of thinking – **problem solving or convergent thinking,** the kind of thinking where there is only one correct answer.

Conventional intelligence tests are confined to the classroom and do not measure the bargaining and economic skills these children possess. Copyright © Popperfoto.

Question – what is the capital of France? Answer – <u>Paris</u>.

Question – as hat is to head, roof is to which of the following

<u>flower</u>, <u>whisky</u>, <u>house</u>, <u>computer</u>, <u>dog</u>.

Answer – house. A hat covers a head just as a roof covers a house.

To get the right answers requires **convergent thinking** because the question converges or focuses on one answer.

The psychologists who first worked with IQ assumed that a key element of intelligence was the ability to tease out verbal and logical similarities and differences. That's why IQ tests often have so many questions of this sort:

In what ways are cows and horses alike?

or

As dog is to bark, cat is to flea, nap, paw, purr.

The IQ test soon came to be divided into a series of tasks as psychologists were convinced that there were different abilities to test. Classic IQ tests like the Stanford Binet make it possible to extract measures of **verbal IQ**, **numerical IQ**, **spatial IQ** and **performance IQ**. **Musical IQ** is sometimes also tested.

Typical IQ questions

Verbal IQ

1. Find a word that can go into the bracket and make a word with all these SC (…), T(…), B(…),SP(…)

2. Komala monoharm means 'a lovely lotus' in Sanskrit; tadage vartati komala means 'the lotus is in the pond'. What is the Sanskrit for lotus? What is the Sanskrit for lovely?

Numerical ability

3. Fill in either plus or minus signs in this sequence:

   $3\ 2\ 3 = 8$

   $11\ 6\ 8\ 4 = 9$

4. What are the next two numbers in this series?

   7, 11, 9, 14, 12, 18

Spatial Ability

5. What should the next picture in this series be?

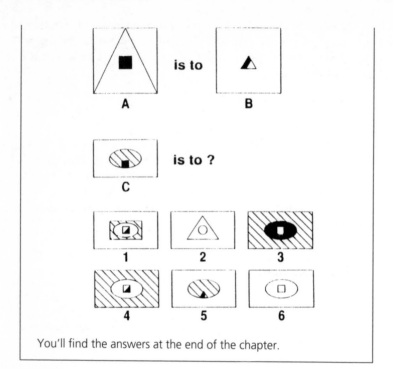

You'll find the answers at the end of the chapter.

When does IQ start?

One of the most impressive findings about IQ scores is their stability over time. If your IQ at 10 years of age is 122 it is likely to be much the same when you are 40.

Correlations between scores on IQ tests at age 2 to 3 years and later scores are low, however. It's only after the age of 6 that IQ scores stay very stable. The Cambridge psychologist N.S. Mackintosh (1999) suggests this is evidence in favour of the environmental or nurture position. Experiences, good or bad, stimulating or the opposite, in the first six years affect intelligence. There is also little correlation between the scores of babies on IQ tests and the best-known infant ability tests, the Bayley scales (1969). Yet the Bayley scales test many of the kinds of task Piaget observed, such as grasping for objects and looking for objects.

Cultural bias

In theory, IQ tests probe pure intelligence. But it's actually not that simple to frame questions which do not depend on some knowledge. Even a question such as

as bee is to flower, dog is to

television, chewing gum, bone, jam, tree

assumes some knowledge. Only if you know that a bee generally sucks the pollen out of a flower will you realise that bone is the right answer because dogs chew and suck on bones.

Some intelligence tests even carry anagrams which require very particular kinds of knowledge. The following question is for adults:

LAID, GRITMETA, THERATCH, SITMASE, SAPISCO. All of them bar one is a famous artist. Name the exception.

The answer is Theratch because the others who have been scrambled are Dali, Magritte, Picasso and Matisse. Theratch rolls out as Thatcher. To get this question right requires not just verbal dexterity but some knowledge of Western art and culture. And if you're an art lover, you may be less good at the next question. Who is the odd man out – and why?

GANKEE, SURGEONRF, WEON, THERATON, LEDHOD

Keegan, Owen, Hoddle, Ferguson are all in football. The answer is Theraton at which unscrambles into Atherton, who is a cricketer.

Cross-cultural confusions

Psychologists like cross-cultural work. What can be nicer than getting a grant to see how kids in Singapore do IQ tests? In the last 40 years, there has been considerable work on IQ tests in different cultures but it is very hard to come to any clear conclusions.

In the 1960s, controversial evidence was put forward showing that black Americans did significantly worse than whites on IQ tests. Some argued this was genetically caused; others that it reflected the poorer environment of most black children – and the fact that IQ tests had been designed by whites for whites.

Ironically, white Europeans score less well on tests than Japanese and Chinese. It has been claimed that Eastern children do better because they have to learn to recognise the immensely complicated Chinese and Japanese letter symbols which requires great attention to detail. In a recent study Flaherty (1997) compared the scores of 72 Japanese university students with those of 52 Irish students on a task often used to test visuo-spatial IQ – the Group Mental Rotation Test. This is one of those tests where you have to recognise what a squiggle or a complex shape will look like if rotated 45 or 90 degrees. The Japanese students outperformed the Irish significantly. One difficulty is that Flaherty didn't look at motivation – and some researchers claim the only reason Eastern children do better is that they are more motivated than Western children to show they do well.

To make it harder to know just what is happening, Flaherty notes an Australian found that aborigine children do better than Europeans on visuo-spatial tasks too – and aborigine kids in 1981 certainly weren't learning Japanese letters.

There is also evidence that people from different cultures interpret the instructions given in tests very differently. In an entertaining set of studies Cole *et al.* (1971) gave Nigerians questions from IQ tests. On the whole, the Nigerians did poorly but when the researchers asked them to answer these questions as stupid people would, they did much better.

The issue of comparisons between races and across cultures is difficult scientifically and politically sensitive. It is clear there are differences between blacks, whites, Chinese and Japanese but it remains hard to be sure why.

In an attempt to get beyond these cross-cultural issues, some researchers have tried to find what is the most basic measure of intelligence there could be.

Eysenck has suggested it is speed of processing information to address this problem.

Intelligence is just quickness of mind

A set of lines are presented in an instrument called a tachistoscope and subjects have to press a button if they see it. The time it takes to make a motor response (pressing the button) can be subtracted from the time it takes to make the decision as to whether or not the lines are there. People with high IQ will report the line being there correctly when it is shown for much shorter periods than those with low IQ.

Eysenck looked at **reaction time** studies where there seemed to be a correlation between reaction time – the time it takes to respond to a stimulus – and IQ. Second, Eysenck looked at inspection time studies where there seemed to be a correlation between **inspection time** – the time it takes to 'notice' a stimulus and some of its features – and IQ.

The correlations were negative, Eysenck claimed. The higher the IQ, the quicker or less the reaction time (RT) or inspection time (IT).

Again these studies seemed to point to a close link between heredity and intelligence because speed of processing would seem to be so fundamental. It seems, however, Eysenck and others were too optimistic. In his IQ and Human Intelligence (1999) the Cambridge psychologist N.J. Mackintosh has reviewed the question of correlations with such basic biological measures.

Mackintosh (1999) writes 'two simple behavioural measures, reaction time and inspection time have been found to correlate with I.Q.' These correlations are in the order of –0.20 to –0.30 for RT and –0.25 to –0.50 for IT. Mackintosh argues neither reaction time nor inspection time tasks 'can be regarded as pure measures of the speed of information processing'. Worse, RT and IT aren't measuring the same thing. He concludes the correlation between IT and IQ is not a correlation with 'g' but probably with a factor of perceptual speed, of how fast the brain processes information from the senses. This may be related to intelligence but it is something different from intelligence. Research on this issue is ongoing.

Motivation and personality

Many critics have argued that IQ scores don't just reflect cultural awareness but personality and motivation.

I had personal experience with my youngest son. We wanted to get him into an oversubscribed kindergarten in south London. We were invited for an interview. Age 30 months, he did the puzzles presented to him and then blithely informed the kindergarten teacher 'this is my exam'. He was immediately accepted. Whatever his scores on the puzzles, he had showed he was very astute for his age.

If people who do well on IQ tests do so because they are better motivated or more persistent, one would expect them to outperform those with a lower IQ on any test requiring persistence and concentration.

Scores on tests like digit span and rote memory for nonsense syllables correlate in the order of 0.30 with IQ. Mackintosh (1999) argues this is a lower correlation than might be expected if persistence counted for so much.

Personality and temperament also seem to have a much smaller relationship with IQ. Petrill and Thompson (1993) gave IQ and achievement tests to 163 children together with measures of six aspects of personality and temperament. Achievement and IQ correlated 0.46, achievement and temperament correlated only 0.25 and IQ and temperament only 0.14. Allowing for the contribution of achievement to both IQ and temperament, the actual correlation between IQ and temperament was just 0.02, i.e. it was more or less a matter of chance.

Mackintosh suggests that whatever may account for different scores on IQ tests, it is not personality. Personality and motivation may well influence success in life but it doesn't seem that crucial in IQ test performance he argues. Some psychologists, however, claim the opposite – that personality is crucial.

Paterson (1999) presented a paper at the London Conference of the British Psychological Society in which she reported a five-year study of innovative engineers. She argued strongly that tests of competence tended to ignore issues of emotion and personality. She found that engineers who were good at devising novel solutions – an instance surely of applied intelligence – tended to be much more challenging. They tended to agree with the statement that it is better to ask for forgiveness afterwards than to ask for permission beforehand, and that is a matter of personality!

Virtue and IQ

Despite evidence that being clever doesn't make you good, we tend to identify intelligence as a sign of worthiness. Mackintosh (1999) argues strongly against this view, stating 'intelligence is not synonymous with virtue. Ranking people by their IQ score is not the same as awarding them badges for varying degrees of merit. Some people are too clever by half, or too clever for their own, or anyone's else's good.' Mackintosh also argues that 'banal platitudes', such as saying honesty and integrity matter as much as IQ, 'really ought not to need saying but much writing about IQ tests, especially that from IQ testers themselves, has often appeared to imply that IQ and general worth are one and the same thing. They are not.'

All these criticisms mean that measuring cognitive development has to go beyond IQ.

Divergent thinking

Many questions in real life do not have one correct answer. Psychologists have tried to study this by seeing how people answer questions such as how many uses you can think of for a brick. You could quite sensibly answer – to build houses, to build walls, to stand on, to prop windows open, to sling at the police when rioting. This requires what psychologists call **divergent thinking**. Instead of focusing on the one right answer, the good divergent thinker comes up fluidly with a whole range of possibilities.

Many psychologists equate divergent thinking with creativity but divergent thinking is not so much a question of creativity as of fluidity. First, there are wrong answers to the uses of a brick test. If someone said one use of a brick was as a snack, they would be loopy, poking fun or just wrong. Secondly, how do you judge whether someone who comes up with 15 uses of bricks is really more creative than someone who comes up with 3 good ones? It depends on the quality of the answers.

The following comes from real answers to another object in the uses of objects test:

Would you think Alfred and Annabel are equally creative?

Annabel's six answers: I can use a matchstick to light fires, to pick my nose (disgusting), to build model boats, as a wedge, as a toothpick, to illustrate the fact that a line is the shortest distance between two points.

Alfred's answers: I can use a matchstick to light a coal fire, to light a stove, to light the kettle, to light a bonfire, to light a candle, to burn a hole.

Alfred, a would-be arsonist perhaps, can see only one use for a matchstick – to light things. He isn't really producing divergent thoughts. Annabel's uses are more varied which shows she has more truly divergent uses for a match. But both subjects score 6 uses.

The most sensitive tests may, however, not be much use in some situations. Children may not be motivated or, if they are clever, they may resent the very nature of the test and do poorly. The British psychologist Liam Hudson, in his *Contrary Imaginations* (1966), studied teenagers doing A levels in British schools. They all had to choose whether to do arts or science subjects. An arts specialist would do English, French and history; a science specialist maths, physics and chemistry.

Case history: Liam Hudson's creative kids

Liam Hudson gave some of the tests of divergent thinking to gifted arts and science A-level students. He was surprised by the results. The arts specialists did well on the tests of divergent thinking but many of the science specialists did not. They scored high on convergence yet they were very creative. One boy called Spinks was 17 and building a computer that would optimise the speed of model cars racing round a track.

Spinks was imaginative and yet his responses to the Uses of Objects test were few and predictable. For barrel, he said to hold beer in, stand on it and roll along, to stand on. For paper clip he said use as an electrode or use as a spring. Hudson struggled to find an explanation for this. He concluded that the Uses of Objects test bored Spinks.

Hudson's research alerted psychologists to the difference between fluid thinking and really creative thinking such as writing a short story or doing a drawing or devising a new computer. It's much harder to measure that kind of creative cognitive skill.

An interesting confirmation of Hudson's ideas comes from the biographies and autobiographies of great scientists like Einstein, Newton and the physicist Richard Feynman. All three seem to have arrived at solutions intuitively. All these men studied invisible forces that worked at the level of both subatomic particles and galaxies – hard stuff to visualise.

Einstein said that his gift had nothing to do with mathematics but in 'visualising effects, consequences and possibilities'. Newton had, according to John Maynard Keynes, the 'peculiar gift' of 'holding in his mind a purely mental problem until he had seen right through it'. Feynman had 'a physical picture of the way things happen and the picture gave him the solution directly with a minimum of calculations'.

How many minds are at home? The work of Howard Gardner

In the last ten years a different approach to cognitive development has come out of America.

Psychologists such as Howard Gardner and Robert Ornstein claim that we have not one brain but a whole set of modules or components that sometimes work together and sometimes compete for executive action. Gardner works at Project Zero at Harvard University. The Project studies how children develop – and especially how they develop creatively. He has mocked the pretensions of the IQ tests. He told me that they had been designed to pick who would be a top-class colonial administrator and know how to file instructions from London or Paris while sipping gin in the middle of the tropics. (Gardner interview in Cohen 1995)

Multiple intelligences

Gardner claims there are seven different kinds of intelligence: linguistic, logical mathematical, spatial, bodily kinaesthetic, musical, interpersonal which we use to understand others, and intrapersonal, which we use to understand ourselves.

Gardner and his colleague Robert Ornstein have devised a complex model on this basis. They argue there are many separate, semi-autonomous 'modules' in the brain. Ornstein calls these modules multi minds; Gardner calls them multiple intelligences. Sometimes they work together; sometimes they compete. In any individual, one set of modules will be more developed than others. One should not be asking the question of whether people are more intelligent but how bright they are on modules A, B, C and so on.

The notion of modules has become influential. The very word modules has been influenced by this kind of psychological theory.

To test the cognitive development of a child means, Gardner argues, testing each of these intelligences separately. There is no logical reason why a child should not score very high on some intelligences and very low on others – and the intelligences don't have to develop at the same pace.

Gardner's seven intelligences.

Case history: autistic child artists

Gardner makes much of children who have one skill to an unusual degree – and who may lack other vital skills. He described the case of a child artist called Nadia who had a remarkable ability to draw horses but was otherwise borderline autistic. Another well-known artist is Stephen Wilshire who suffers from autism. His verbal IQ is average and his intrapersonal intelligence is low but his visual memory is so acute he can view a building fleetingly and reproduce it years later with remarkable skill

Drawings by 5-year-old Nadia who is autistic (left) and an average 6.5-year-old (right). Reproduced with permission from L. Selfe (1976), An autistic child with exceptional drawing ability. In G.E. Butterworth (Ed.), *The child's representation of the world*. New York: Plenum Publishing Group.

Conclusion

It's important to be aware of the pitfalls of measuring cognitive development because it isn't just an academic exercise. Important life choices and chances depend on how well children do on tests. Access to higher education in the Western world depends crucially on how well children do because it is assumed that measuring intelligence predicts how well people will do in later life. There is much evidence to suggest that other factors like personality and motivation also matter in terms of evaluated success. In a Western culture that has become more showbiz-dominated there is another factor which may affect success – sheer luck. Take *Who Wants to be a Millionaire*, the TV quiz. No one can have total general knowledge and so able contestants are often stymied by questions that just don't fall into their orbit of knowledge. One young woman who was doing well had to answer a question about a 1970s less-than-brilliant soap. She smiled that she was hardly born when it was on. The role of luck in success is something psychologists have not even started to consider.

Exercise in self-observation

Go back now to the test set at the start of this chapter. Has what you have read altered your view of your own intelligence or intelligences – and if so why?

Answers to the questions;

1. ORE as in SCORE, TORE, BORE, SPORE

2. 3+2+3 = 8

   11–6+8–4=9

3. Komala = lotus

4. Monoharm = lovely

5. The answer is 2

Useful reading

Gardner, H. (1992) *Multiple Intelligences*, New York: Basic Books.

Hudson, L. (1966) *Contrary Imaginations*, Harmondsworth: Penguin; lively case studies of creative children and why their cognitive development does not fit simple theories.

Kline, P. (1990) *Intelligence*, London: Routledge; excellent primer by an author who favours IQ.

Mackintosh, N.J. (1999) *IQ and Human Intelligence*, Oxford: Oxford University Press; technical but thorough account of the latest data and controversies.

8

Nature or nurture?

Introduction

Philosophers and scientists have debated whether intelligence, personality and creativity are gifts we are born with (a matter of nature) or skills that we learn (a matter of nurture) for centuries. From the Greeks onwards, doctors and philosophers claimed individual personality was determined by the humours. People tended to be one of four types – the choleric, the melancholic, the phlegmatic or the earthy. Physiological characteristics accompanied each type. If you had black bile, for example, you were likely to be melancholy. Personality was determined largely by biology.

In this chapter we're going to look at:

- **methods of looking at nature *v.* nurture**

- **social class and IQ**

- **can vitamins boost IQ?**

- **does pollution affect IQ?**

- **can we teach children to be more intelligent?**

- **the genetics of genius**

- **the mystery of why IQ scores are rising**

- **the inheritance of personality traits**.

Once upon a time, philosophers like John Locke and psychologists like John B. Watson claimed newborns were a *tabula rasa*, a blank tablet. This 'blank' babe had nothing innate. She or he could be shaped, trained, conditioned, moulded by reward and punishment into any kind of creature – tinker, tailor, actress, salesman, waitress, don, athlete, fraud.

Watson and Locke's position was always controversial. Now, it has fallen out of favour as a result of the rise of genetics. The discovery of the DNA (deoxyribonucleic acid) and its double helix structure in 1954 led to a new science of genetics. One surprising finding is that for all our differences, 97 per cent of every human being's genes are also to be found in all other human beings.

In the past few years, geneticists have announced the discovery of genes for certain aspects of intelligence, creativity, schizophrenia, getting fat, keeping thin and much else besides though there have often been debates around these claims. Schizophrenia, for example, does have a large genetic component but not all psychiatrists accept there is a gene for it. Some diseases like cystic fibrosis have been shown to occur because of a single gene defect. It would be astonishing if the way we think and our cognitive development were not enormously influenced by our genetic make-up.

In this chapter, we're going to focus on the 3 per cent of genes that differ from person to person. This small proportion of genes will make one person a blonde, another a redhead, one person green-eyed, another blue-eyed. These genes will also contribute to making one person extrovert and another introvert, one clever, one stupid.

Separating nature and nurture

Working out how much of any characteristic is due to nature or genes and how much is due to nurture or learning is not that straightforward. Just where do genes end and the environment begin? For each baby, the womb is the first environment. For 9 months babies eat and drink what their mothers provide. If the mother smokes, consumes alcohol or is a crack addict, the foetus will be affected in the womb. Mothers who smoke during pregnancy give birth to smaller babies whose IQ is lower at 4 years of age.

Is this a genetic or an environmental effect? Ernst et al. (2001) have traced studies which show that in Canada at least babies born to mothers who smoked are more likely to end up as juvenile delinquents 16 years on. Puff now – pay later. The mother's smoking is an environmental variable which influences the baby's biology before birth. But it may also be linked to class and parenting style.

The actual calculation of how much is nature, how much is nurture, is complicated by the phenomenon known as **regression to the mean**. Statistically, intelligent parents will have more intelligent children than less intelligent parents but the children will, as individuals, tend to be closer to the average score for intelligence than their parents are. They 'regress' to the mean or the average score.

To work out the influence of nature and nurture, one needs to understand not just genetics, statistics and psychology but rather more improbable areas such as social work practice. Social work practice dictates how children are adopted. Adopted children – especially pairs of twins where one is adopted and the other is not – are an important source of data for the nature *v*. nurture debate.

Twins who have grown up separately are an important source of data in the nature *v*. nurture debate. Copyright © Linda Sole/Photofusion.

Throughout the twentieth century there have been projects which have tried to follow the lives of twins and, especially, twin pairs where one stays with the biological family and the other is adopted. The practical problems of doing this research, keeping in touch with all

151

the twins in the samples, are great. One of the most thorough of these projects has been run by Robert Plomin who headed The Colorado Twin Project in the 1980s and early 1990s. Plomin now works in London at the Institute of Psychiatry.

The subject of nature *v.* nurture is emotive. IQ tests arouse passions so researchers often draw exaggerated conclusions from limited data. Worse, some classic studies that favour the nature position have involved fraud. There are concerns that the nature position justifies discrimination against some ethnic groups and that couples will increasingly choose to have designer babies. The final and, perhaps, most astonishing twist is that for centuries, scientists have believed enough data would give a final answer. When we knew enough, we could declare, for example, that nature was 70 per cent responsible and nurture 30 per cent responsible for a child's cognitive development.

Some of Plomin's recent research suggests we may never be able to pin down a final score in such a neat way. The contribution of genetics and environment may vary at different periods in someone's life.

Progress exercise – self-analysis

As in the rest of the book, try to relate this to your own personal experience. Think of your own parents, your brothers and sisters. If you come from a stepfamily, think of your 'extended' brothers and sisters.

In what ways do you think you're like your parents? Do you see any characteristics you have inherited from your grandfather, for example? Do people tell you that you're just like he was – good at maths, say?

Make a list of any of these apparently inherited characteristics.

Make a list of skills and traits you seem to have but no one else in your family does. For example, if you're good at dancing, does anyone else in the family shine on the ballroom floor?

If you are a twin, list the ways in which you think you are very similar to your twin – and list the differences.

Methods of studying nature *v.* nurture

Scientists have developed many methods to tease out the role of nature and nurture. Assessing the value of these methods is an important step in trying to understand the debate. There are two main research strategies scientists have used.

Twin studies

Twins either are **Monozygotic (MZ)** or **Dizygotic (DZ)**. MZ or identical twins come from the same egg which split in two before fertilisation. DZ or fraternal twins started out as two separate eggs which both got fertilised and shared the same womb.

MZ twins share the same genes completely, DZ twins are as genetically similar as brothers and sisters which is why they are called fraternal twins. They are 'closer' insofar as they shared the same uterine environment. If you compare how MZ and DZ twins score on different tasks, you get some measure of the role of heredity.

The ideal cases are identical twins who are separated and brought up by different families. Since the twins have been brought up in different environments, the extent to which they are alike will give a pure measure of the influence of heredity.

Studies of children who have been adopted

If the IQ scores of adopted twins resemble those of their biological parents that suggests the influence of heredity is higher. If their scores resemble those of their adoptive parents that suggests the role of the environment is more important.

Changes in IQ due to experiences

If intelligence is largely a matter of biological heredity, it should not be easy to boost. There is a 30-year history of compensatory programmes which have tried to improve the IQ scores of, nearly always, disadvantaged children. These include the American Head Start programme which offered poor children early teaching and more recent nutritional programmes. The Nobel Laureate Linus Pauling believed vitamin C improved IQ. If intelligence is largely a matter of heredity, these interventions should not work too well. The consensus till recently has been that these often well-intentioned and expensive programmes don't produce very significant improvements. It is too early to judge the Sure Start programme in Britain.

The Burt saga

Fraud has complicated the debate, however. After Galton, the debate on intelligence and heredity was largely dominated by a British psychologist Cyril Burt (1883–1971). Burt was the chief educational psychologist in London and still publishing papers in the 1960s when he was in his late 70s. Burt had no doubts. Intelligence was largely inherited.

Burt published studies based on the IQ scores of identical (MZ) and fraternal (DZ) twins. The data seemed to show identical twins had very similar IQ scores even when they were brought up separately. In other words, intelligence was largely a matter of heredity.

Real life is more complex than theory though. When one twin can't be brought up in the real biological family, social workers, families and adoption agencies often look for another family that is as similar as possible. If twin A is the son of a doctor, they'll try to place twin B with a doctor's family. Often when both twins can't stay with their biological family, close relatives will take the other twin. Usually the parents will choose relatives who are as like them in terms of class, education, even personality style as possible. What appear, in theory, to be two completely different environments may not be that different in fact.

If the twins brought up in families of relatives have very similar scores, some of that will, of course, be due to heredity but some may be due to the fact that they have actually been brought up in similar environments, homes where, for instance, there are plenty of books and parents help with the homework. Twins brought up in families that are total strangers to each other are rare.

One of the reasons Cyril Burt's work seemed so important was that he followed over 100 sets of identical twins brought up in totally unrelated families. According to N.J. Mackintosh (1999) there have been only 162 such sets of twins studied in 90 years of research. Lynn (1997) points out there have only been four papers apart from Burt's on identical twins reared apart. They are prized subjects, the gold dust of research.

Burt published correlations between these twins in the late 1930s, in 1955 and 1958 and again in 1966. The correlations for the IQ scores were between 0.92 and 0.94 in the IQ for monozygotic twins and 0.62 for dizygotic twins. In his 1966 paper, nearly half the correlations Burt reported were identical to three decimal places with correlations he had published previously. In other words, these correlations were incredibly stable. Incredible is the word. Normally correlations do vary. It has been argued psychologists should have spotted how strange these unchanging correlations were.

No one suspected the very respectable Professor Burt of the unforgivable sin of faking his data. Despite the too perfect correlations, both Hans Eysenck and Arthur Jensen relied on Burt's data to support the idea that intelligence is 69 per cent heritable, i.e. that genes influenced over two-thirds of the IQ score. Eysenck's faith was specially odd; he knew Burt and did not like him. 'Burt was an ever hostile power threatening to make academic life in England difficult or impossible for me,' Eysenck wrote in his autobiography, *Rebel with A Cause* (1990).

In 1974, the American Leon Kamin argued Burt's data could not be relied on. No study could really turn up such positive unchanging correlations. At the same time, a journalist on *The Sunday Times* Dr Oliver Gillie discovered that no one seemed to know where the co-authors of Burt's 1955 and 1958 papers were. Massive international publicity didn't turn up any clues to their whereabouts. Gillie concluded Burt had made up these co-authors to make his findings seem more authentic.

In his excellent book *The Burt Controversy* (1995) Mackintosh convincingly argues that Burt probably did fake some data – and concedes that this data is crucial to the heredity case.

Mackintosh has noted 'Leaving aside the question of how far Burt's data were actually fabricated, an issue of wider import is why they were treated with such respect for so long. It did not take a particularly careful inspection to see that they were inadequately reported and riddled with error. It is tempting to see evidence of a hereditarian conspiracy.'

Mackintosh argues it is not safe to use any of Burt's data. But there have been other well-controlled and honest twin studies since then, such as Robert Plomin's Colorado Twin project, a 60-year-long study of Swedish twins and a further study of 45 twin pairs led by Thomas Bouchard, a colleague of Plomin's. In all these studies the correlations for the IQ scores of monozygotic twins reared apart were high. Bouchard's sample was 0.79, for instance.

Studying the children in adoptive situations has provided useful confirmation. If heredity counts more than environment, adopted children should not become too much like either of their adoptive parents because the biology will out. The evidence suggests that this is true. Studies of the IQ scores of adopted children show a correlation of 0.32 between stepbrothers and stepsisters with different biological parents who are brought up in the same family. Put crudely, one can attribute a third of their intelligence to the environment.

The decreasing influence of the environment

But Plomin (1998) has also found that the environment does have an impact on intelligence and a curious one in terms of time. We saw earlier that there is a critical or imprinting period for certain behaviours – especially language. Children of different biological parents reared in the same home will tend to have closer IQ scores between the ages of 7 and 14 than later on. It is as if environmental influences are at their height between 7 and 14. After that, on average, children revert to being closer to the score of their natural parents. By a person's mid twenties, there is no correlation in the IQ scores of adopted children brought up in the same family. I stress on average as there are bound to be many individual exceptions.

Plomin admitted being astonished because one would expect the environment to keep on influencing one more through the years. He argues it may be that very intelligent people develop different habits. Between 7 and 14 children have to go to school. They're forced to read, do maths, use their brains. But once they leave school, everything is up to them. Intelligent young adults, Plomin suggests, will read more and think more. Many may even find it necessary to reflect once a day on Descartes' Cogito. So we have a circle. The genetic make-up of intelligent people leads them to behave in ways that will reinforce their intelligence.

Plomin's unexpected finding – in terms of brain structure it suggests a development between 7 and 14 which is then in some cases stalled or even reversed – illustrates the complex relationship between nature and nurture in the matter of intelligence.

Is social intelligence also inherited?

Lynn (1997) reports a study of 100 twins born in Galway – of whom 33 were MZ and 67 were DZ. They were studied between the ages of

3 years 10 months and 6 years 7 months. Unusually the twins were also given a test of social intelligence – the Vineland Social Maturity Scale.

Lynn found heredity accounted for less of the verbal IQ score than expected. Other IQ scores – numerical and spatial – fitted well with Plomin and Bouchard's figures. Lynn also found that 0.30 of the variance on the social intelligence scale was due to hereditability. He says this is the first time anyone has reported on the genetics of social intelligence and suggests 4- to 6-year-olds learn more of their social skills than their cognitive skills from their parents.

The heredity score

The ambition of finding out what proportion of intelligence is due to heredity and what is due to environment is giving way slowly to an understanding of how complex the issue is. Getting to grips with the figures can seem daunting but given how vicious the controversies involved have been one ought to try to do it. It seems that those nature enthusiasts Eysenck and Jensen got it a bit wrong. They suggested that heritability accounts for 69 per cent of intelligence. Plomin suggests that 0.48 heritability is probably about the right sum for intelligence, which means it accounts for about 50 per cent of intelligence. The make-up of that 50 per cent is not simple, however. It consists, according to Chipuer *et al*. (1990), of

G a additive genetic variance 0.32

G n non-additive genetic variance 0.19

Plomin argues that twenty years ago it was just about feasible to argue there was no major genetic component to IQ because of the Burt fraud and the controversy sparked by it. Today, he claims it would be impossible to maintain that because of both his own Colorado Twin Project and research that has stemmed from that.

Class and the role of parents

There are opposing arguments that point to the importance of environment. IQ has been associated with social class ever since the question has been asked. Terman (1916) found a difference of some 16 IQ points between the average for social class 1 children (upper-class and professional) and social class 5 (unskilled working-class and un-employed) children. A study of 15,000 British children in 1958 found a difference of 17 IQ points between children in these social classes. This could mean that children of richer families are exposed to a more favourable environment but it could equally mean that they inherited 'better' genes for IQ from their wealthier (and presumably more intelligent) parents.

Recently there's been some controversy about whether parents really do contribute to a child's IQ. A number of old studies suggest fairly strongly that what 'every parent knows' is true. Majoribanks (1972) interviewed the parents of 200 Canadian boys and got data on their social status, occupation, attitudes to achievement and intellectual develop-ment. He found substantial differences between working-class and middle-class parents. He also found that parental attitudes correlated more strongly with children's IQ scores than did parental status. Attitudes lead parents to treat their children differently. For example, Bradley *et al.* (1977) found correlations as high as 0.77 between IQ and measures of the home environment. These included how many play materials there were and the mother's involvement with the child. Again, the socio-economic status of the parents mattered less, it was their attitude.

In 1998, the American psychologist David Cohen caused some controversy, however, claiming parents have no impact on the intel-ligence of children. He is not a hard-line geneticist but argues that peers have much more to do with cognitive development. It's difficult to accept this argument partly because of the results outlined above. What is clear is that the relationship between parents and the intel-ligence of their children involves both heredity and parental attention. The key questions include:

Do parents who read more to their children improve IQ by providing a better environment?

Or do children whose genes make them brighter insist their parents read to them more?

Scarr (1997) has argued that there is a genetic part to these correlations. She has devised a model which factors out the genetic contribution and claims to find, once that is done, little evidence of parental contribution to IQ. Mackintosh (1999) pokes some fun at the attempt of behaviour geneticists to argue that while the environment does influence IQ, it has nothing to do with parents. Parents make up much of that environment. The results of Lynn (1997) also suggest parental influence matters.

Class and vitamins

Nutrition is also an issue that has been raised in connection with IQ. Some studies in the Third World suggest that children who suffer from malnutrition do score lower on IQ tests. This is hardly surprising. In the developed West, relatively few children are malnourished and those who are will also be victims of many other disadvantages. More interestingly, there is some evidence that good nutrition can boost IQ.

A small study of 30 Welsh children (Benton and Roberts 1988) triggered interest in this area. The authors gave the children a vitamin and mineral supplement for 8 months. Control groups either got nothing or a placebo. At the end of the 8 months, the experimental group scored 10 points higher on non-verbal IQ. Replications haven't been totally successful. In one case, the effect was only on certain non-verbal test scores. Eysenck and Schoentaler (1997) offer a rather optimistic view of these results claiming that even when the results weren't statistically significant, they were at least always in a positive direction.

Eysenck, the great advocate of the heredity position, told me in one of the last interviews before his death that he had been astonished by the vitamin studies. 'We tested a group of perfectly average normal kids. This was a study that involved the nutritionist John Yudkin and the Nobel Laureate Linus Pauling . . . There was after three months an 11 point rise in IQ. After a year the rise was still there. If you can improve the IQ of city kids this is important. I was absolutely thunderstruck.' (Cohen 1995) One of Eysenck's most endearing characteristics was the way he sometimes felt he had to react because he had been clobbered by the evidence.

Contemporary culture likes the idea of boosting brain power. Some drug companies are toying with cortical cocktails that will increase your brain power; they are supposed to stimulate the production of certain neurotransmitters.

Pollution also affects IQ. Studies in Scotland and Australia show that children who are exposed to more lead in the atmosphere will tend to have a lower IQ.

Psychobabble and brainpower

We also live in a culture where many people want to use psychological techniques to better themselves. Self-help books that claim to improve your memory and your brainpower fill the bookshops. Among the best known are Tony Buzan's *Mind Map* and Edward de Bono's books on lateral thinking. It may be useful to study your own attitude to studying.

So a little self-analysis.

Self analysis

What techniques do you use when you want to make sure you understand something?

Swotting?

Trying hard to master the task?

Do you believe that the effort you make makes a difference?

Can we teach intelligence?

The question shouldn't be controversial. Good schools teach children how to learn. Yet because of the nature *v*. nurture controversy, many experts claim that attempts to boost intelligence by tinkering with the environment are doomed to failure.

Pessimism about this came out of long-term follow-ups of American 'compensatory education' programmes like Head Start and the pre-school Perry project which tried to give disadvantaged children a richer environment. Head Start did give pre-school children an immediate boost of up 7.5 IQ points. The Perry project did even better. It initially gave young children a real boost with average IQ scores in a very 'weak' group surging from 80 to 95. Until the age of 8, the children did remain ahead of the control group but from then on, there was no effect on either reading or mathematical skills. The Perry children were rated as more socially competent and they were less likely to be seen as needing remedial help but this was hardly a triumph.

Recently, neuropsychologists have warned that there is little evidence two years on for the magical effects of giving children under the age of 3 varieties of stimulation.

Nevertheless one series of studies with teenagers shows it is possible to boost scores on tests that have many similarities to IQ tests – Scholastic Aptitude Tests (SATs).

American universities require students to take the Scholastic Aptitude Test in order to gain places. These are tests of verbal and numerical ability as well as specialist subjects. Questions are multi-choice, not essays. In the 1960s, organisations that coached students for these SATs sprang up. In 1971, the College Examination Board denounced these coaching institutions. Stanley H. Kaplan, who headed the largest test coaching organisation in America, questioned the basis of the research. In 1979 the Federal Trade Commission released the results of a ten-week coaching period at one of Kaplan's institutions. They showed a significant boost in verbal and mathematical skills.

Psychologists were not convinced so the immensely prestigious Educational Testing Service assessed his schools. The results were strange. In two schools there was only a small rise but in a third school students showed a hefty rise of between 20 and 35 points in verbal and mathematical scores. All this suggests that one can learn the skills needed to do better at tests very close to IQ tests. The critics claimed that all students were doing was learning the skills of taking tests and that this doesn't mean they had become more intelligent.

Since the only way of judging intelligence is by taking tests, this wasn't a very intelligent critique.

The mystery of the rise in IQ

The most curious fact about IQ, however, is that it has been rising throughout the twentieth century. In 1933 and 1947, the Scottish Council for Research in Education reported on the IQ scores of nearly all the 11-year-olds in the country and found IQ scores had risen between 2 and 3 points over the two years. In France and the Netherlands data are available for nearly all 18-year-olds because they are tested when they start national service. Between 1950 and 1980, IQ scores increased an average of 20 to 25 points. Studies in Japan suggest the rise has been even greater there.

Mackintosh raised the question of whether these increases might be due to the fact that more children are middle class but a re-analysis of the Dutch data showed that no more than 30 per cent of the increase could be attributed to this. Mackintosh also doesn't believe it has anything to do with the increased period of time children spend in education. One particular oddity of this data is that the greatest increase is not in verbal IQ but in non-verbal IQ, especially spatial IQ. I will argue in Chapter 10 that this may be partly the result of an increasingly sophisticated visual culture in which we live. Any contribution to the nature *v.* nurture debate needs now to solve this particularly thorny problem.

Genius

I also want to look at an extreme example of the relationship between genetics and achievement because it shows how the nature *v.* nurture argument may not be a useful way of looking at a special form of cognitive development – genius.

Plomin shows in detail how the influence of genes is additive. He suggests there may be exceptions, though, when it comes to genius and he invokes an idea called **emergenesis**.

We saw earlier that Galton, author of *Hereditary Genius*, believed genius was very much a matter of nature. Though Eysenck often followed Galton he argued in one of his last books *Genius* (1995) that Galton was wrong in this. Galton was a snob and was seduced by Victorian elitism, the idea that the best families sending their children to the best schools, were bound to produce the best, most creative brains. True genius does not run in families, argued Eysenck. Rather, it surfaces in the unlikeliest of places.

Genius is not of genius born, to paraphrase Shakespeare whose own family was nothing special. Shakespeare's father was a puffed up tradesman who wanted to be mayor of Stratford. You can breed fast horses but it seems you can't breed composers, writers, painters, scientists and mathematicians of genius.

To stop his own preconceptions contaminating his sample, Eysenck looked at the family backgrounds of the 28 greatest ever mathematicians as chosen by E.T.Bell in his *Men of Mathematics*. He found little evidence of mathematical ability in the families of these 28. Fermat's father was a leather merchant; Pascal's a minor civil servant who didn't allow him to read mathematics books; Gauss's father was a peasant; Monge's a peddler. The Bernoullis were the only family with any history of mathematical creativity. One out of 28 is the exception that proves the rule.

Case history: Indian peasant to Cambridge don

'My favourite example is the Indian mathematician Ramanujan,' Eysenck wrote. He was born in 1887 in south India into a poor family. His mother was convinced of his mathematical genius but she did not want him to go to school. 'The environment did everything possible to discourage him which is fairly typical,' Eysenck sniped. At the age of 18, the young Indian dropped out of the University of Madras having failed his high school diploma. For the next 5 years, he drifted, fell ill, did not find work. His fortunes only changed when he met the founder of the Indian mathematical society who was astonished by his notebooks.

Three years later, Ramanujan wrote to G.H.Hardy, a British mathematician at Trinity College, Cambridge. Hardy invited him to Trinity and the two worked together for the next four years. Ramanujan is reckoned to be one of the most magical and intuitive of all mathematicians. But he was certainly not related to any eminent men. At the age of 32, Ramanujan fell ill and returned to India. He died a few months later.

In music, again, genius does not seem to run in families, not even in the Bach family. Although the sons of Bach included talented composers, none of them really ranks among composers of genius as father Bach did.

Galton's mistake, Eysenck believes, is that he thought genius followed a normal statistical distribution. Galton calculated that 400 people in every million were 'idiots' and that 250 achieved great eminence. Galton divided the idiots into 120 so-called light idiots who were below average and a further 280 true idiots. Galton believed the same kind of figures were true of genius.

Eysenck argues that every million human beings does not produce 280 true geniuses. True genius is very rare if you define a genius as someone who makes a lasting contribution to a field. Newton, Einstein, Shakespeare, J.S. Bach, Beethoven, Rembrandt had genius. History is full of writers and scientists who were important in their time but whose work now seems dated and is not much read or played. Galton's normal distribution may fit eminent men with high IQs and real talent but genius is much rarer.

Eysenck claims there are surprisingly few arguments about who is and who isn't a genius. He points out roughly 250 classical composers have their music played today. But the work of just sixteen composers accounts for half these performances. These are the geniuses – Beethoven, J.S.Bach, Mozart, Haydn, Chopin, Verdi. But no one puts Telemann in that league. (I wish in that last interview I had asked Eysenck if he thought Freud was a genius. Almost certainly not. Yet Freud made a lasting mark and his books sell sixty years after his death.)

The fact that genius does not form part of a normal distribution is a key part of Eysenck's theory. It leads to his claim that genius is more or less a genetic accident, a freak or the result of what Plomin calls emergenesis. To understand that freak better, Eysenck suggests we need to look at three factors – cognitive style, psychiatric symptoms and our growing knowledge of brain biochemistry.

Since Aristotle, writers have said madness is close to genius. There certainly is a large genetic component in schizophrenia. Eysenck argues some individuals are born prone to produce more of the neurotransmitter dopamine and less serotonin. They are more likely to be schizophrenics. But in a few of these individuals that doesn't happen; rather a combination of independent polygenes leads to a huge quantitative change. This is emergenesis, the freak or the miracle. This combination makes it possible for geniuses both to have unlikely, even mad, creative associations and to have the critical acumen to weed out the too bizarre and useless ones. Eysenck argues this is the root of genius. It has nothing to do with family inheritance; 'emergenesis' is, almost literally, a freak.

Eysenck's theory shows there is no way of manufacturing geniuses. It is all down to the genes continuing to throw up freakish or miraculous combinations. True genius is almost entirely a matter of biological luck but nothing to do with the family. It's a view Plomin seems to accept – and an interesting example in any nurture *v.* nature essay.

Personality

One of Plomin's collaborators, Thomas Bouchard, has also studied the inheritance of personality. Bouchard looked at five key traits – neuroticism, openness, amiability, extraversion and emotionality. He relied on some of the data that had been collected by Eysenck and concluded that about 40 per cent of the variance in the personality scores was due to heredity. In other words, personality is not as biologically based as intelligence but genetics still help make us our characters. This would hardly have surprised the Greeks who devised the theory of the humours.

Conclusion

The traditional way of framing the nature *v.* nurture debate is now antiquated because we are much better able than before to quantify how each contributes to cognitive development and to personality But while many results point to the importance of genetics, one must not forget Cutting and Dunn's evidence that class affects the rate at which children develop a theory of mind.

Further reading

Anthony Storr (1974) *The Dynamics of Creation*, London: Allen Lane.
David Cohen and Stephen MacKeith (1991) *The Development of Imagination*, London: Routledge.
H.J. Eysenck (1995) *Genius*, Cambridge: Cambridge University Press.

9

Cognitive development in the classroom: Reading, writing and arithmetic

Introduction

One of the most obvious places to study cognitive development is the classroom. It's been estimated children will spend 15,000 hours in class before the age of 16. In the nineteenth century a high master of the famous London school St Pauls wrote to parents to say that the only subjects they taught were Greek and Latin. Children had three half days off a week. Parents were quite free to use the time to engage tutors to teach their offspring other subjects but, as far as the school was concerned, all one needed for a proper education was the classics.

Education has changed out of all recognition since then – and it has been heavily influenced by Piaget and his ideas. Yet I suspect Piaget would have approved of the eccentric stand taken by St Pauls. In 1930 Piaget became director of the International Bureau of Education which was the forerunner of UNESCO. In Britain in the 1960s, Piaget started to influence teacher training enormously.

Yet, rather curiously, Piaget did not have a great deal of faith in formal education. He thought the ideal teacher was better employed creating the conditions in which the child could mature rather than in teaching subjects on the curriculum. (Maybe Piaget had had a few sadist, lighted-match-flinging teachers too.) For Piaget it was important to offer the child the chance to handle objects, to do practical work, as it was through these actions the child would learn. For Piaget that was

We will spend 15,000 hours in the classroom before the age of 16. Copyright © Popperfoto/Reuters.

the key phrase: 'the child would learn' rather than the child being taught.

Piaget wrote: 'It is a great mistake to suppose that a child acquires the notion of number and other mathematical concepts just from teaching. On the contrary, to a remarkable degree, he develops them himself, independently and spontaneously' (Piaget 1953).

Piaget was always making fun of Americans who wanted to know how his theories would help devise ways of pushing children to learn more, younger and quicker.

Today, Piaget's ideas seem rather other-worldly though, as we shall see, they fit in well with the concept of progressive, child-driven education that is now unfashionably radical in Britain. Schools are under more scrutiny than ever before to prove children are performing well in very traditional ways.

Falling standards

Since the 1980s, successive British governments have been worried by poor standards of literacy and numeracy, by tabloid stories of 16-year-old kids 'graduating' from school barely able to read and write and by even worse horror stories of first-year undergraduates having to be given remedial classes.

Between the ages of 4 and 14, children are now assessed on 8 scales covering reading, writing, speaking and listening, mathematics and personal and social development. The Basic Skills Agency in a study in 1996 painted a gloomy picture, however. They found under 20 per cent of the population managed, for example, to answer correctly 12 simple mathematical questions. Such results encourage the government to test more and more often in the hope of driving up standards.

The Department for Education and Employment assume these tests are useful in three ways. First, they make it possible to judge how well a particular child is doing and, at 14, whether or not they deserve to go on to further education. Second, test scores should identify a child's weaknesses and so offer individual help. Third, the scores tell parents which schools are good and which are best avoided. The government hopes teachers in bad schools will be motivated to try harder. Teachers often argue the government's standards don't allow for the fact that schools in poorer areas are dealing with children who are disadvantaged.

Charles Desforges, head of education at the University of Exeter, recently told *The Independent on Sunday* (28 February 2000) that studies in the United States made him worry about the impact of constant testing on children. Some children came near the bottom and 'that does lead to a great deal of anxiety and alienation and depression'.

Progressive *v.* formal

Animals can be trained to perform the most extraordinary feats. In the nineteenth century a horse called Clever Hans was thought to be able to count and solve arithmetical problems. It turned out the horse responded to some very clever signals from his trainer. Studies of chimps show they learn neither to count nor to read. With normal children, these skills come naturally given normal social interaction with parents and, eventually, teachers. This raises an intriguing question. If we want animals to do anything remarkable we have to train or educate them but do we actually need to teach children formally at all? Untaught, would they learn anyway?

Educational practice has nearly always been influenced by grand philosophical positions. One can very roughly see two positions emerge over the last 300 years – **the progressive and the formal**.

There are progressives like the French philosopher Jean Jacques Rousseau (1712–78) who believed, as we have already seen, that the child was a noble savage and shouldn't be disciplined or forced to learn. Rousseau wanted children to flower. His ideas influenced educational philosophy more than educational practice. No school today offers children such total freedom though Summerhill in Suffolk, set up in 1938 by A.S.Neill (1888–1973), has come close. At Summerhill, children only go to lessons if they want to. They decide a good deal of what they study; they enforce the discipline in the school council. (For an account of the school see A.S. Neill's *The New Summerhill.*)

Neill has had few imitators but his liberal ideas influenced education to some extent. He argued against cramming facts into children. The best education recognised that children are naturally curious and want to learn. It gave them a chance to use their imagination and develop their creativity.

Opposed to this liberal view are theorists who think children need structure and discipline. Such theorists believe children have to be trained, taught and socialised. In a best-selling book published in 1789, *Practical Education*, Mr and Mrs Edgeworth who had fourteen children (and so a lot of practical experience) advocated this position. Children were taught to read from when they were 4 years old. The Edgeworths argued against reading fairy tales to children; children needed facts, training in reading, writing and mathematics.

Assessing success

These conflicting views are reflected in the research that has been done on cognitive development in the classroom. However, it's difficult to measure the outcome of educational interventions and even harder to establish the causes of any differences.

If Class A does better this term is it because: a) they have a new and interesting teacher; b) the schools has finally spent some money buying textbooks so that kids don't have to share; or c) a significant number of kids have stopped skiving off because the local police are now cautioning truants?

Learning to read

Any proper assessment of the impact of psychological theories on education has to examine controversies about reading. There have been complicated debates about what it takes to learn to read. It is a skill that requires a combination of skills. The child has to learn to look at the letters that make up a word long enough to start processing them. It then has to realise that each letter makes up a particular sound – and that sounds make up a word.

In the nineteenth century, children were usually taught to read phonetically. Phonetic means teaching the sounds particular letters made and then teaching how to combine those sounds into a word. So a teacher would split the word BANANA into three syllables BA NA NA and teach the two letters that made up each syllable.

In about 1920, after studies suggested children could do better, a new technique started to be popular in America. It was called 'look and say' or visual retrieval. Instead of being taught the sounds of individual letters and how letters made up syllables, children were first taught to recognise whole words like CAT, DOG, MOON, COW and so on.

The theory was based a little on Gestalt psychology which suggested that people perceive patterns or wholes. Psychologists who study the eye movements involved in reading have found that good adult readers typically fixate on part of a word and then scan forward in what are called saccades (short, jerky movements) to see what is coming next. Recent work reported by Wood and Terrell (1997) suggests that children who are learning to read are much more hesitant in their pattern of looking. They fixate the letters, then scan ahead, then often regress to look at the letters again. The visual skills needed to read can be mastered by the age of 3.

Reading early

There are studies which show children can learn to read much earlier than imagined. Soderberg (1977) presented reading materials to a child from the age of 2 years and 4 months. During the first six weeks, the child was presented with word cards. Then the word cards were assembled into a short book. Over the next three months, the child learned to read 150 words and was acquiring 5–10 new words a day. Soderbergh observed that it was as the child read and re-read the books that she got the intonation and emphasis right. Soderbergh was arguing that children can, in fact, learn to read far earlier than is imagined if they are helped to do so sympathetically.

Jeanne Chall (1983) developed a useful four-stage theory of how children learn to read. The theory is intriguing for cognitive development because it suggests that a key skill is very unexpected.

From birth to 5, children master preparatory skills for reading. Many learn to identify the letters of the alphabet, to write their names and to read a few words. They also tend to be able to identify the logo of their favourite fast food restaurant long before they can read. Children also learn words are made up of letters and sounds and that you can break these up and join the elements up in different ways, so that CAT, for example, is made up of three sounds C, A and T. And here is the surprise.

Chall reports results where 4- and 5-year-old children were told to tap once for each sound in a short word. They were supposed to tap twice for AT – a and t – and three times for CAT. Liberman found that children who scored well on this tapping test tended to read well three years later. Chall argued the results suggested the importance of phonetic talent in learning to read.

If children don't have a natural phonetic talent, usually they can be taught. Bradley and Bryant (1983) showed that training 4- and 5-year-olds in phonemic awareness led to better reading skills. Understanding how words break up into different sounds seems to predict reading ability much better than the ability to recognise letters does. Bryant in a series of studies has emphasised the importance of rhyme production and rhyme detection as predictors of reading skill. Intuitively that makes sense. Children who are taught nursery rhymes do well at reading later on.

Drat, the cat in the hat makes a fuss on the bus, Gus

This is the mystery of the brain. Our ability to read, crucial for most learning, is closely correlated with our ability to break up patterns of sounds correctly which is almost certainly correlated with rhythmical skill. Good writers know this, intuitively making children listen to the sounds of words. Dr Seuss books are especially skilful at that. Take his tale of 'Green Eggs and Ham'.

Would you like it
with a house?
Would you like it
with a mouse?

Recently, however, a very sharp controversy has flared between Bryant, one of the most respected workers in this field, and a team from York University led by Charles Hulme. Hulme and his co-workers argue that Bryant and his colleagues have put far too much emphasis on rhyming skills. Hulme contrasts the ability to identify 'cat' as a word that rhymes with 'hat' with phoneme detection and phoneme deletion skills. You say the word 'blame' to a child and ask what the word would be like if you took away the b. The right answer is 'lame'. That is phoneme deletion. You say the syllable 'ca' to a child and ask what it needs to become the word 'cat'. The child who is good at phoneme detection says 't'.

Hulme has been involved for some years in reading research. A study by Laing and Hulme (1999) found very poor readers learned to read better if they were given training in phoneme skills. This finding may have prompted the study which has led to the controversy between him and Bryant.

Muter *et al.* (1998) tested 38 children over a period of two years. The children were given a series of tests between the ages of 3 years and 10 months and 4 years 3 months. The first test given at this time (Time 1) was an IQ test. The score range of the 38 children was from 90 to 142 with a mean IQ of 114. The children were also given tests of rhyme production, rhyme detection, phoneme identification and phoneme deletion. They were re-tested at the ages of 5 years and 3 months (Time 2) and 6 years and 3 months (Time 3). At those times they were also given standard reading tests.

Muter and Hulme argue that the crucial factors in predicting reading ability have nothing to do with rhyming. At the age of 5 years 3 months, they found a positive correlation between the phonemic skills a child had had at Time 1 and reading skills. Muter and Hulme called these segmentation skills because they reflect the ability to segment words, dividing them into bits like 'b-lame' or 'bo-ne'. One other important factor was letter knowledge, being able to recognise letters. By the time the children were 6 years 3 months, there was a correlation between rhyming skills and reading but Hulme and his colleagues suggest this is much more marginal than the segmentation skills. Children's reading vocabulary at Time 2 was also an important factor in predicting reading skills at Time 3.

Does using rhyme help us learn to read? Copyright © Emily Barney/ Photofusion.

Bryant countered, in the same issue of the *Journal of Experimental Child Psychology*, that Muter and Hulme's work had methodological flaws. When looking at the influence of rhyming, the specific phrasing of the question was to ask children if words 'rhymed with or sounded like' other words. Take three words – 'take', 'bake', 'bike'. 'Take' and 'bake' rhyme but 'bake' and 'bike' also sound alike. They don't rhyme but they have a shared phoneme – 'b'. So by asking about rhyming and sounding alike, Muter and Hulme had not really done a clean test of rhyming skills versus segmentation skills, Bryant alleged.

By now, in the polite parlance of academic psychology, the conflict was sharp. Muter and Hulme then conducted a third experiment with some 30 children. They tested Bryant's claim – and got the results out in time to make the same edition of the *Journal of Experimental Child*

Psychology. They asked children to respond either to choosing a word which 'rhymed' with 'cat' or a word which 'rhymed with or sounded like' 'cat'. They claimed there was no difference between the two conditions and that, therefore, their work was a clean test of the differences between rhyming and segmentation skills. In a clear attempt to cool the passions, Hulme and Muter acknowledged Bryant's huge contribution to reading research. Still, they insisted, on this the master was wrong.

The debate is extremely important both theoretically and in practical terms given that Britain and many other countries still struggle with poor literacy.

It's a debate which focuses on the micro-skills children need to master in order to read. Chall's theory focuses also on the macro-skills.

Automatic Reading

In Chall's Stage 2, children read quite fluently but the process requires considerable concentration. So they find it hard to learn through reading because much of the brain capacity is devoted to the reading task itself. As a result, Chall suggests, children aren't reading to learn and to acquire information at this stage. They are learning to read, not reading to learn.

As reading becomes more automatic, at Stage 3, children can acquire new information through reading because not all of their brain effort is dedicated to the actual process of reading. Material is now integrated with general knowledge.

The next stage Chall proposes is Stage 4 – essentially the secondary school stage when children become effective and critical readers. Chall makes much of the fact that children now come to realise that information can come from many different viewpoints. Just as the 6-year-old has learned that different people have different feelings and opinions, children now come to understand authors have varying ideas.

Only when schoolchildren reach Stage 4 can they play one of the essential academic games – writing the essay. To provide a good answer to 'what were the causes for the defeat of the Spanish Armada?' you have to discuss the following at least – the heroism of Sir Francis Drake, the bad weather, the bad organisation of the Spanish navy, the inspirational leadership of Queen Elizabeth I. Then you put the arguments for making each one more or less of a cause for the Armada being given a bloody nose.

It's important to realise essay writing is a bit of a game – my attitude may just give away my own views about that – but it's a game you can only play once you have reached a certain cognitive stage.

Nicolson *et al.* (1999) have studied children who by the age of 6 have already been identified as having problems with reading. They devised a system for providing these children with extra help – in these days their research focused both on how helpful the interventions were and how cost-effective they were. The extra help consisted mainly of 3.5 hours of extra teacher help and advice to parents to read with their children. Nicolson and her colleagues found that 40 of the 62 problem children were 'accelerated' thanks to the programme.

Overlapping strategies in spelling

In Chapter 2, dealing with Piaget, we saw that Siegler (1996) had developed a critique arguing that Piaget's stage theory underestimated the amount of variability in children's behaviour. Siegler emphasises that children are always changing. He has extended his analysis to reading and what follows implies a critique of Chall's work.

Rittle Johnson and Siegler (1999) in a study of spelling argue that similar conclusions can be drawn from how children in the first and second grade of American schools (aged 6 and 7) learn to spell. They argue earlier studies had stressed first-graders spelt largely by sounding out words and that they then progressed to use a variety of additional strategies, including relying on rules and drawing analogies.

Their current findings, Rittle Johnson and Siegler suggest, make it clear that from the first grade children use more than one rule. In the first grade, children use three strategies on average – mainly sounding out, visual checking and retrieval. In the second grade they used the same three strategies as well as their growing sense of the rules of spelling. The better spellers used more strategies and increasingly so the harder the words were to spell.

The point Siegler is making in general is that it is wrong to think of children progressing from one stage to another in some smooth manner as they master new cognitive skills. The learning of all skills in childhood is very much a matter of trying different things at different times, of flexibility.

Learning to count and do mathematics

By the age of 24 months, many children are starting to parrot 1, 2, 3, 4. Some are starting to count on their fingers. Just as there has been a debate on the best method of teaching children to read, there has been a long debate on the best way to teach children mathematics. Psychologists even manage to quarrel about whether it's good or bad to let children learn to count using their fingers. Some cultures are more inventive than we are. The Oksapmin of New Guinea use a system which involves 27 parts of the body and have a basic set of 29 numbers.

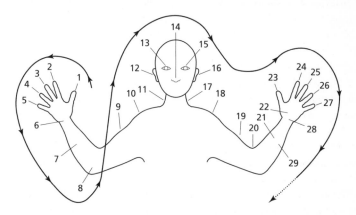

Learning to count. The Oksapmin of New Guinea use body locations to represent numbers. From G.B. Saxe (1981). Body parts as numerals: A developmental analysis of numeration among the Oksapmin in Papua New Guinea. *Child Development, 52,* **306–316. Reprinted with permission of SRCD.**

But what do numbers mean to children?

Many 2- and 3-year-olds do not count reliably beyond three or four but that doesn't mean they 'regard numerosities beyond four and five as undifferentiated "beaucoups"'.

E.L. Thorndike (1932) argued that learning arithmetic was a matter of building up the strength of a large number of what he called habits. By habits he meant the association that $2 + 2 = 4$.

Once a child had built up $3 + 3 = 6$ and $7 + 5 = 12$, these individual islands of learning could fit together 'as a soldier fighting together with others'.

Piaget objected to this approach. He conceded that it was of course possible to teach 3- and 4-year-olds to parrot mathematical tables and, indeed, you could probably get them to parrot more complicated material. But the fact that young children could repeat a text or an equation did not mean the children knew what it all signified. Piaget argued that because pre-operational children had no concept either of number or of multiplication, any mathematical operations they appeared to perform were the product of mere rote learning.

Piaget wrote: 'For the child to be able to combine operations be they numerical or spatial operation, he must have manipulated, he must have experimented, he must have acted, not just on drawings but on real materials, on actual things, on points, on surfaces' (1976).

Not all psychologists were as pessimistic as Piaget, however. While distancing himself from Thorndike, Brownell (1928) argued that children could learn mathematical operations if they were set out in a way that was meaningful to them. Instead of endless drilling through multiplication tables, Brownell recommended using pictures and drawings so that children could see what they were counting or dividing. In a study that Siegler cites, Brownell and Carper (1944) found that when children were starting to learn multiplication they used strategies other than retrieval – i.e. just recalling what 7 multiply 8 is – three times as often on hard problems than on easy ones.

McConnell (1958) compared the two methods of repetitive rote learning and a more 'rounded' approach using pictures and objects as learning aids. McConnell found that the drill was a perfectly good way of teaching children but they could not handle new problems as well as children who had been taught in a way that promoted understanding.

There has been some interesting work on how 6- to 9-year-old kids often make mistakes when subtracting. Often they make errors because they forget some of the basic – and not immediately obvious – procedures.

$$
\begin{array}{r}
307 \\
-182 \\
\hline
285 \\
\hline
\end{array}
$$

Instead of taking 8 away from 10, answer 2, the boy has taken 8 away from 0 and left 8. He's then simply taken 1 away from 3.

The evidence suggests that we reach a knowledge of mathematics partly as a result of experience and partly as result of formal learning (Gelman and Gallistel 1978). Trying to impose the formal learning too soon leads to what Piaget most criticised – parrot learning.

Case and Yakamoto (1996), as part of their attempt to revive stage theories, trained children using a number programme called Rightstart. Children aged 4 to 5 were trained to count objects from 1 to 10 and also, back along the same row, from 10 to 1. They were also shown the relationship between the number of objects set out in two rows. They were then tested on a number of tasks including the Number Knowledge test and the Balance Beam test. In the latter test, children are shown a beam which is stacked with weights at each end and balanced on a fulcrum. Props keep the beam still.

Children are asked to predict which end will go down when props are removed and to explain their judgement.

Children who had been through the Rightstart programme were much more proficient at this task, doing twice as well as a control group. Case and Yakamoto argue that Piaget was just too dogmatic about the uselessness of specific teaching because if children can explain why one beam will go down, they are well beyond the rote learning or parroting Piaget despised.

The evidence suggests that while it is usually helpful for children to learn at their own pace, education doesn't have to be quite so passive. Children can be trained and pushed and still learn properly.

But the child has access to different ways of learning maths. Siegler has also tried to inject his ideas into the study of how children learn mathematics. He has conducted a number of experiments which show that in dealing with addition, for example, 4- and 5-year-olds are inconsistent and use strategies which include counting on fingers, putting up fingers without counting them, counting out loud and retrieval when trying to solve simple addition problems. The easier the problem the more children relied on retrieval; once sums were as hard as $4 + 3$, they tended to use the more complex strategies. In a study of multiplication, there was a strong correlation among 7-year-olds between the use of complex or back-up strategies as opposed to retrieval and the errors they made. Siegler's fundamental point is that children are not stuck in a stage where they have to attack a problem one way but they use different methods precisely because their state of cognitive development is fluid.

As children become faster and more expert at skills, they may prefer to use the method that works for them but it's not inevitable. Siegler's model of cognitive development challenges the accepted stage view profoundly because it presumes children have access to more than the one way for that stage to tackle various problems.

New theory

It's a measure of the fragmentation of the field that one new theory which uses some of Piaget, some of Vygotsky and some original thinking sits a little at odds with the rest of the field, not because, like Siegler, it challenges it but because the author seems to talk a slightly different language. Kieran Egan is an American who, like Howard Gardner, has built up something of a following. In his book *The Educated Mind* (1999) he outlines a theory of development which is not only intriguing but has clear implications for how children are taught in the classroom.

Egan suggests children and young adults develop through a series of stages, again. Egan places great emphasis on the Western cultural tradition because he believes that as children learn to read and write, the material they absorb and create affects the way their minds develop. In this he resembles Vygotsky. But Egan isn't just talking about the usefulness of social contact in learning. He suggests the mind is receptive at certain stages to particular forms of story and learning.

The first of Egan's stages, the Somatic, is much like Piaget's sensory motor period. But with the second stage, Egan takes a new line. Egan argues that this second Mythic Period (roughly from ages 2 to 8) is a time when children have an intense love of fantasy and start to understand narrative or story-telling. The individual slowly assimilates the major traditions of Western cultures. Children build an early sense of the world around certain organising principles that are usually opposites. They divide the world into good or bad, love or hate, fear or security just as in fairy tales. This is one of the responses Vygotsky lamented they lost around the age of 7.

Between the ages of 8 and 15, Egan sees a Romantic understanding develop. One characteristic is plotting the limits of human experience and transcending the limits of conventional everyday experience. After 15, children will become more at ease in dealing with abstract thoughts and will then graduate to Irony. (Cultural gurus currently believe Ironic is the flavour of the age.)

Conclusion

Given the enormous interest in cognitive development it is perhaps surprising there is less research in the classroom than in the home. The election of a new Labour government in 2001 has led to even more emphasis on improving the classroom performance of children. It seems likely that we shall soon see children assessed every year of their school life. Though some children will get very stressed by these tests, the research suggests that Piaget was probably too dogmatic in his insistence that children should not be pushed.

Thinking matter

Many of those who read this book will have to deal with children in a learning situation. The arguments centre on Piaget and Vygotsky still. Piaget believed children had to mature to learn. Vygotsky thought children could be helped by sympathetic teachers and peers. Egan provides a less familiar theory which is gaining converts in the US.

10

Television, toys and the child as consumer

I started this book talking of airheads and of being brain-dead. Having looked at much serious research, I now want to playfully explore a few 'wild' ideas. The ideas may well be wrong but might also provoke some thoughts. In this chapter I'm going to look at:

- **information bombardment and children**
- **the influence of television, computers and computer games**
- **are children getting smarter?**

It's a long journey from Descartes' Cogito to the computer games, websites and multimedia packages of today. If Descartes were alive and cogitating now, however, I suspect he'd be very interested in the impact of computers and playing e.games. Descartes likened the brain to the hydraulic fountains that were hi-tech in his time; today comparing the brain to computers is the rage, the neural web mirrors the global web.

You don't have to buy the hype that went with campaigns like 'Do not underestimate the power of Playstation' to believe the media children are exposed to from birth must have some effect on them. Remember Piaget's key notions of assimilation and accommodation. The infant brain has never before been bombarded with so much information to assimilate.

The average American child spends over 20 hours a week watching television, He/she will have seen over 1,600 murders by the age of 6 – and in addition will have seen reports of hundreds of real murders where neither the act of killing nor bodies are shown. Millions will have seen the horrors of the attack on the twin towers on 11 September 2001. Children as young as 3 are familiar with video games.

The media child is not just a passive recipient of information, a cognitive couch potato.

One can hardly blame Piaget for not mentioning television. It wasn't much of an influence in Geneva in the 1920s. Yet I want to suggest that television is affecting aspects of child development in many ways – and some of these are hard to identify because they are subtle and involve what I should like to call knowingness. English philosophers distinguish between knowing that and knowing how. I know *that* Descartes devised 'cogito ergo sum' – a specific piece of knowledge, while I know *how* to drive a helicopter, a skill. But there is another sense of knowing. If I say a person is knowing I imply they are unusually self-aware, that they have a sense of the context and culture. To be knowing is more than just to know. To be knowing is to be critical, to be alert to the ironies in a situation.

It seems to me that children's television now assumes children become knowing quite young. Take two examples – the cartoon series *The Flintstones* and *The Simpsons*. *The Flintstones* came 30 years before *The Simpsons* and both series offer an ironic take on American lower-middle-class suburban life. But many of the jokes in *The Flintstones* are simple. In Stone Age suburbia, they had dinosaur mobiles instead of cars; their clothes were a Marks and Spencer's version of loincloths. *The Simpsons* offers far more subtle ironies about family relationships and personalities. They make fun of adult pretensions in a way children can grasp.

Kinder (1993) has done in-depth work on such themes. She observed how her child watched cartoons from the age of 2. Kinder approached the subject from a different background – that of studies of how children interact with media. Media studies accepts that we live in a global village where images and information bombard us all day long. Fact, fiction, news, sport, fantasy, advertising, game shows – a variety of genres all of which have to be understood.

The average American child spends over twenty hours a week watching television. Copyright © Gary Simpson/Photofusion.

Kinder studied how her son watched a number of children's shows and analysed the surprisingly complex demands that some of them made on their toddler audience. She highlights an episode in the cartoon series *Garfield*, an episode called 'Eating Fellini'. In this episode Garfield is discovered by an egomaniac Italian film director called

Federico Fettucine who is not the kind of a man to make spaghetti Westerns. The film is accompanied by the soundtrack to *8½* which was directed by an egomaniacal Italian film director, Federico Fellini. His film, *8½* is about his inability to make a film. In the cartoon Garfield wants to be the star of the film but he has been cast as the stunt double. Garfield manages, however, to take over the film. He changes the film, usurps the role of director.

Kinder observes that some episodes require the child to understand not just visual punning but the difference between different styles and genres of film. This is, I would suggest, part of acquiring knowingness. In one episode Garfield is trapped in the wrong end of a cathode ray tube. He becomes trapped inside a television – and a very modern television at that. The TV keeps changing channels so that in quick succession our cat hero is caught in a football game, *Swan Lake*, a cowboy film and becomes a bargain item in a used pet shop.

The most TV-literate child won't get the references to Fellini but Kinder observed that children did get many of the basic jokes – and certainly grasped all the frantic genre and style switching in the last episode I described. Kinder also talked to her son about what they were seeing: she was an active parent in her viewing. In terms of involving parents television is curiously interactive. There seemed an understanding of the ironies, of the subverting of authority.

Computers and kids

British schools have been using computers since the 1980s. The use of computers requires concentration and manual dexterity. There has been surprisingly little research on the impact of using computers on how children think. We know from consumer studies that many children have access to the Internet and use it. The University of London library lists only six books related to that topic – and all of them date from the 1980s. This is a rich area to explore.

There has also been an interesting interplay between the findings of psychologists and products for infants and young children. Toys have become far more interactive. In *The Rational Infant* (1989) Tom Bower commented on the fact that toys and baby products had changed radically over twenty years. When he first had children in the early 1970s, toys and strollers seemed designed for a passive baby. By 1989, most baby products presumed the baby was active and needed stimulation. Early Learning Centres, for example, offered parents toys and games that would help toddlers acquire skills and learn.

You could sneer that these were products for anxious pushy parents who wanted their children to succeed in order to do better than Next Door. It could also be argued more positively that these new products allow children to explore, to experience more, in fact, to do all the 'handling' Piaget would have wished them to have to give their brains the chance to mature.

Since 1989, the 'market' for babies and young children has continued to evolve. There is now a veritable industry aimed at turning the child into a consumer. It has been estimated that the child market in the USA is worth $64 billion a year. The consequences of this are both good and bad – children are exposed to choices as never before but they are also exposed to pressures.

I want to look at one of the central debates that this has provoked because it does have implications for cognitive development – the vexed question of children and advertising.

In March 1999 a major European conference called Kidpower was held. Its subject was on how to sell to children. The conference was chaired by the professor of psychology at Exeter University, Brian Young. Attended by many leading players in the kids' market such as toy manufacturers Lego, Fisher Price and the Cartoon Network broadcaster, the conference offered a guide on how to unlock the hearts of kids through marketing. Specific sessions dealt with how to grab kids' attention, for example the use of colour and graphics to attract kids. There were focus groups for 4-year-olds and even some advice on how to frame ads so that kids will pester parents to buy toys.

There has been an enormous amount of research into the question of children and television advertising. Conservative psychologists argue that children should not be exposed to advertising because they do not really understand what the aim of the advertising is – to make them buy. Others, often commissioned by industry, claim that children today are much more media-literate than psychology has allowed. Two questions dominate academic research. First, how old are children when they realise ads are different from programmes? Second, how old are children when they grasp ads aren't neutral but trying to sell? These questions aren't just academic. Greece and Sweden currently have banned television advertising aimed at children. Advertisers in Britain and other Western European countries don't want the ban to spread.

The consensus is that by the age of 5 most children know ads aren't normal programmes. (One recent study put it at 79 per cent of 5-year-olds). But while young children spot the genre is different, many psychologists claim they still don't get the commercial motive. There are arguments about what's a proper test of whether children are 'fully aware' of the purpose of advertising.

Jeffrey Goldstein of Utrecht University points to 25-year-old 'widely cited research' which found 96 per cent of 5- to 6-year-olds, 85 per cent of 8- to 9-year-olds and 62 per cent of 11- to 12-year-olds 'do not fully understand the purpose of TV advertising' (Ward, Wackman and Wartella 1977). But Goldstein asks if their test wasn't too stringent. Kids had to explain verbally ads were trying to sell and make money out of them to be 'fully aware'. This is exactly the kind of question Piaget would expect a child to answer, at the earliest, in late concrete operational stage.

When this research was done, the global village was a quiet place. It had yet to explode with niche channels, 24-hour cartoons and good-for-all-ages shows like *The Simpsons*. It's possible that it took longer for children to get wise to the purposes of advertising in the media-innocent 1970s and 80s.

I want to look at three pieces of research, all of which reinforce the idea of the media-literate child that Kinder dealt with. Brian Young showed 66 children aged 4 to 8 years old two sorts of ads – the genuine article and doctored ads. The doctored ads had unusual punch lines. One ad showed a face cream. The genuine version extolled a face cream with the punch line that it made you better-looking; the doctored version praised the cream but the punch line was it gave you disgusting spots.

Children were shown both versions, asked which they preferred – and why. Four- to five-year-olds liked the funny endings better and didn't notice whether or not the punch lines made commercial sense. The reactions of 6-year-olds were different. Just over 50 per cent understood there was something wrong with the funny endings but often couldn't say what; just under half responded like the younger kids.

All the 8-year-olds were totally familiar with the advertising game. They laughed at the doctored ads – not just because they were funny but because they were pathetic as ads. A face cream that gives you spots is not a product you'll sell, they pointed out.

Glen Smith, director of the Children's Research Unit which does work for the advertising industry amongst other clients, thinks children who are much younger understand the nature of advertising. He told me of a study where he had shown commercials to children aged 4. 'We had dolls representing children, mum, dad and so on. We asked the children to move the doll the ad was talking to forward. We found if there was a frozen pea commercial they moved the mum forward, if it was a toy they moved the child doll forward.' Proof for Smith that young kids understand the nature of advertising because they know who the sales pitch is aimed at.

Smith, however, hasn't published this research because, like much of the Children's Research Unit output, it's confidential and only available to clients. No one can be sure how robust it is. A little paradoxically, while Smith thinks advertising to children isn't 'sinful or wicked' he also told me one should 'be mindful of the gullibility of young children'.

A third piece of research goes further. In Wales, Merris Griffiths has found older children to be not merely knowing but dismissive. Her work for her Ph.D. thesis has not yet been published. In an interview for the *New Scientist*, she told me: 'I started showing groups of 7- to 11-year-olds ten selected ads for toys.' In all she used ten ads – three for girls' toys, three for boys' and four neutral ones.

The children rejected the ads. Griffiths added: 'They felt insulted by them. The girls had the most hostile reactions. They were totally cynical.' This was as true of the 7-year-old girls as of the 11-year-old girls. 'They'd say things like this is trickery,' she said. The extent of the cynicism surprised her.

Media consultants accept the critical awareness of today's children. Nicky Buss of the advertising agency Ammirati Puris Lintas reports 7-year-olds watching the Burger King 'Lost Worlds' ad which uses glove puppets. One carped: 'Why's that man got his hand up a sock. Don't they know how to do it properly? That's not going to get me to buy it.'

Some people may view Kidpower with distaste. Young children shouldn't be manipulated by advertising. I understand where that comes from but our concern to protect children should not make us blind to social developments. There are industries that aim to entertain and inform children. Primary schools in England, for example, welcome girl bands who give free concerts in school. The schools like the free music; the bands use it as a way of getting publicity. Costly ad campaigns include focus groups which get children to talk about how they see products.

Ironically all these attempts to sell to and exploit children culturally may also be having beneficial effects, beneficial effects that research often plays down.

The changing nature of television

Research into the effect of television on children is now nearly 40 years old in the UK. The literature has been almost wholly critical. We have had dire warnings that children who watch TV will lose their minds, become violent and go mad. It's a re-run of Victorian vicars on masturbation.

The first programme to really seize on the educational potential of television was the American *Sesame Street*. *Sesame Street* was produced by the Educational TV Workshop based in New York which was always keen on research. They tested new segments of the programme by filming children watching the programme.

Young *Sesame Street* viewers learned to recognise letters and numbers and had better vocabulary than those who did not watch it. Yet even *Sesame Street* has been attacked because it has cuts about every 30 seconds on the grounds that children's attention span is short.

A recent study of imitation discovered that babies and toddlers found it harder to imitate an action they had seen on TV than one they saw in real flesh. The psychologists found that 15-month-old children could imitate a simple action an experimenter demonstrated with a puppet but if they were shown the action to imitate on TV, they could not do it. By 24 months, however, the toddlers were able to imitate what they saw on TV. The authors speculate that it is not till 24 months that babies learn to accommodate to the basics of TV – that they are seeing an image and that the image is of a different size to real life. But after 24 months they understand that 'grammar' of images. Though they do not say so, their results seem to suggest that after 24 months children can learn from TV – and may learn very rapidly once they understand that television pictures represent reality (Barr and Hayne 1999).

Gunter and McAleer (1990) review research which lambasts television in a variety of ways. Children who watch more television are more stupid than those who do not; 45 per cent of 8-year-olds do not realise that the people taking part in films are actors; few children retain anything they hear or see in so-called educational programmes.

Some children who see violence on TV are likely to imitate the antics of their heroes. The medium is trash and ought to be trashed.

In the midst of this fine outrage no one in Britain asks whether there might be any cognitive benefits to watching TV programmes which don't have an obvious educational intent. In theory, television offers much of what the growing brain seeks – constant stimulation, new images, new sounds. They may be unreal but they're just the kind of stuff the neurones should lap up.

Gunter and McAleer report one study which offers dramatically different results but they comment little on it. It claims that up to the age of 11, children who watch more television are more intelligent than those who watch less. Gunter and his colleague offer no explanation of this finding though they admit to being intrigued by it. This is one of those baffling findings that do not fit conventional wisdom. The other one that strikes me is the finding that non-verbal IQ in particular has been rising throughout the twentieth century.

I'd like to offer an interpretation of these though I must stress it's an interpretation of the wild – but maybe fruitful – guesses sort.

Television and its images do inform and stimulate the brain. Until the age of 11 (at least at the time Gunter was doing this research) children that young did not have a separate TV-set in their own room and watched with their parents. Their brains were stimulated by TV and they talked about what they saw.

After the age of 11, however, pressures to do homework increase, some children withdraw more and more into their rooms. Now the children who watch more TV don't do their homework and may even tend to become much more isolated and obsessive watchers of TV. They become teenage couch potatoes and doomed to exam failure.

I said that this was a chapter in which to explore wild ideas. I don't claim the above is right but it is a hypothesis worth thinking about in the context of a few odd results and the rise in non-verbal IQ.

Into the twenty-first century

In exploring the latest research on cognitive development, I have tried to stress the impact of social, cultural and technological changes. Our means of communication are changing faster than ever before. The child's brain is bombarded with more images, more choices than ever before.

I have suggested there is evidence children are becoming psychologically aware younger than used to be assumed. It's not clear if the reason is that earlier psychologists didn't ask the relevant questions or that children are changing. A combination of the two is probably near the mark.

We are also seeing a shift away from stage theories to a new emphasis on detailed and very specific studies of small behaviours that emphasise both the individuality of children and their psychological maturity. It is too soon to tell whether Siegler's notion of overlapping waves will replace Piagetian and revamped Piagetian stage-theory approaches but Siegler has hit on something in stressing that children's behaviour is quirkier and more variable.

Developmental psychologists need to tread a fine line – seeking to understand both the basics of cognitive development and looking at how the changes we are living through affect the way children think. Psychology has to respond rapidly to social and cultural changes or it will lag far behind what children now do, think and feel. That is one reason it is such an interesting field.

Thinking matter

In any consideration of the applications of cognitive theory, its use by companies selling goods to children is significant.

Throughout this book I have argued that children face a much more competitive environment intellectually than in the past. The same goes for students. If you have been reading this book to pass exams, take small risks. The best marks will go to those who do not just regurgitate what research has found but who have absorbed the trends and underlying patterns behind that research. Don't be frightened of your own creativity, of putting your points of view as long as these are grounded in a good understanding of what experiments have discovered.

References

Andrews, G. and Halford, G. (1998) 'Children's ability to make transitive inferences', *Cognitive Development* 13: 479–513.

Baddeley, A. (1997) 'Short-term and working memory', in E.Tulving and F.Craik (eds), *The Oxford Handbook of Human Memory*, Oxford: Oxford University Press.

Baillargeon, R. (1993) 'The object concept revisited; new directions in the investigation of infants' physical knowledge', in C.E. Granrud (ed.), *Visual Perception and Cognition in Infancy*. Hillsdale, NJ: Erlbaum.

Baron Cohen, S. (1995) *Mind Blindness*. Cambridge, MA: MIT Press.

Baron Cohen, S. and Frith, U. (1985) 'Does the autistic child have a theory of mind?', *Cognition* 21: 37–46.

Barr, R. and Hayne, H. (1999) 'Developmental ability to imitate from television', *Child Development*, 70: 1067–81.

Bartrip, J., Morton, J. and de Schonen, S. (2001) 'Infants' responses to mother's face', *British Journal of Developmental Psychology*, 19: 219–232.

Bartsch, K. and Wellman, H. (1995) *Children Talk About the Mind*, Oxford: Oxford University Press.

Bayley, N. (1969) *The Bayley Scales of Infant Development*, New York: Psychological Corporation.

Bell, E.T. (1928) *Men of Mathematics*, New York: Simon and Schuster.

Benton, D. and Roberts, G. (1988) 'Effect of vitamin and mineral supplementation on intelligence', *Lancet*, 1: 140–44.

Bivens and Birk (1990) 'A longitudinal study of development in elementary school of child private speach', *Merrill Palmer Quarterly*, 36; 443–63.

Boden, M. (1979) *Piaget*, London: Fontana.

Bouchard, T.J. Jnr (1997) 'IQ similarity in twins reared apart, findings and responses to critics', in R.J. Sternberg and E.L. Grigorenko (eds), *Intelligence, Heredity and Environment*, Cambridge: Cambridge University Press.

Bower, T.G.R. (1973) *Development in Infancy*, San Francisco: W.H.Freeman.

Bower, T.G.R. (1989) *The Rational Infant*, New York: W.H. Freeman.

Bradley, L. and Bryant, P.E. (1983) 'Categorising sounds and learning to read', *Nature* 301: 410–21.

Bradley, R.H., Caldwell, B. and Eldaro, R. (1977) 'Home environment, social status and mental test performance', *Journal of Educational Psychology* 69: 697–701.

Bradmertz, J. (1999) 'Precursors of formal thought', *British Journal of Developmental Psychology* 17, 61–81.

Brownell, W.A. (1928) *The Development of Children's Number Ideas*, Supplementary Educational Monographs no. 35.

Brownell, W.A. and Carper, R. (1944) *Learning the Multiplication Combination*, Duke Studies in Education no.7, Durham, N.C.: Duke University Press.

Bruer, J. (2001) *Critical Periods*, New York: Free Press.

Bruner, J. (1972) *Beyond the Information Given*, London: Allen and Unwin.

Bryant, P. (1972) *Perception and Understanding in Young Children*, London: Methuen.

Bryant, P.E. (1998) 'Sensitivity to onset and rhyme does predict young children's reading: a comment on Muter, Hulme, Snowling, and Taylor (1997)', *Journal of Experimental Child Psychology* 71: 29–37.

Bryant, P. and Trabasso, T. (1972) 'Transitive inferences and memory in young children', *Nature* 232: 456–8.

Buzan, T. (1998) *The Mind Map Book: Radiant Thinking the Major Evolution in Human Thought*. London: BBC Books.

Case, R. (1995) *Intellectual Development: A Systematic Reinterpretation*, Orlando, FL: Academic Press.

Case, R. and Yakamoto, Y. (1996) *The Role of Central Conceptual Structures in the Developement of Knowledge and Thought*, Chicago: University of Chicago Press.

Ceci, S., Ornstein, P. A. and Loftus, E. (1998) 'Adult recollections of childhood abuse: cognitive and developmental perspectives', *Psychology, Public Policy, and Law* 4: 1025–51.

Ceci, S. and Bruck, M. (1999) 'The suggestibility of children's memory', *Annual Review of Psychology* 50: 419–39.

Chall, J. (1983) *Developing Literacy in Adults and Children*, London: Pergamon Press.

Chipuer, H.M., Rovine, M.J. and Plomin, R. (1990) 'LISREL modelling; genetic and environmental influences on IQ revisited', *Intelligence* 14: 11–29.

Chomsky, N. (1977) in an interview in D. Cohen, *Psychologists on Psychology*, London: Routledge.

Churchland, P. and Sejenowski, T. (1994) *The Computational Brain*, Boston, MA: MIT Press.

Cohen, D. (1977) *Psychologists on Psychology*, London: Routledge.

Cohen, D. (1995) *Psychologists on Psychology*, 2nd edn., London: Routledge.

Cohen, D. (1997) *Carl Rogers*, London: Constable.

Cohen, D.B. (2000) *Stranger in the Nest*, Chichester: John Wiley.

Cole, M. and Gay, J. (1971) 'The Cultural Context of Learning', New York: Basic Books.

Conway, M. (1988) *Autobiographical Memory*, Cambridge: Cambridge University Press.

Cox, R.R. and Griggs, R.A. (1982) 'Everyday attention', *Psychology News* 28.

Cutting, A. and Dunn, J. (1999) 'Theory of mind, emotions and understanding', *Child Development* 70: 853–65.

Damon, W. (1977) *The Social World of Childhood*, San Francisco: Jossey Bass.

Dasgupta, S. (1998) interview in *Looking to the Future*, video produced by *Psychology News* for the Lord Chancellor's Department, Selborne House, London SW1.

de Bono, E. (1990) *Lateral Thinking*, Harmondsworth: Penguin.

de Botton, A. (1998) *The Romantic Movement*, London: Picador.

Descartes, R. (1634) *Discourse on the Method*, available in Penguin Classics.

Donaldson, M. (1978) *Children's Minds*, London: Fontana.

Dunn, J. and Cutting, A. (1999) 'Theory of mind, emotional understanding, language and family background', *Child Development*, 70: 853–65.

Egan, K. (1999) *The Educated Mind*, Chicago: University of Chicago Press.

Ernst, M. Moolcha, E.T. and Robinson, M. (2001) 'Behavioural and neural consequences of prenatal exposure to nicotine', *Journal of the American Academy of Child and Adolescent Psychiatry*, 40: 630–41

Eysenck, H.J. (1979) *The Structure and Measurement of Intelligence*, New York: Springer Verlag.

Eysenck, H.J. (1995) *Genius, the Natural History of Creativity*, Cambridge: Cambridge University Press.

Eysenck, H.J. (1997) *Rebel With a Cause*, London: W.H. Allen.

Eysenck, H.J. and Schoentaler, J.J. (1997) 'Raising IQ level by vitamin supplementation', in R.J. Sternberg and E. Grigorenko (eds), *Intelligence, Heredity and Environment*, Cambridge: Cambridge University Press.

Fischer, K.W. (1987) 'Relation between the brain and cognitive development', *Child Development* 58: 623–32.

Fivush, R. (1998) 'Children's recollection of traumatic and non-traumatic events', *Development and Psychopathology* 10: 699–716.

Flaherty, M. (1997) 'The validity of tests of visuo-spatial skills in cross-cultural settings', *Irish Journal of Psychology* 18: 404–12.

Flavell, J.H. (1962) *The Developmental Psychology of Jean Piaget*, Princeton, NJ: Van Nostrand.

Flavell, J.H. (1992) 'Cognitive development, past, present and future', *Developmental Psychology* 28: 998–1004.

Flavell, J.H. (1999) 'Cognitive development', *Annual Review of Psychology* 50: 21–45.

Flavell, J.H. and Wellman, H.M. (1997) 'Metamemory', in R.V. Kail and J.W. Hagen (eds), *Perspectives on the Development of Memory and Cognition*, Hillsdale, NJ: Erlbaum.

Flavell, J.H., Green, F.L., Flavell, E.R. and Grossman, J.B. (1997) 'The development of children's knowledge about inner speech', *Child Development* 68: 39–47.